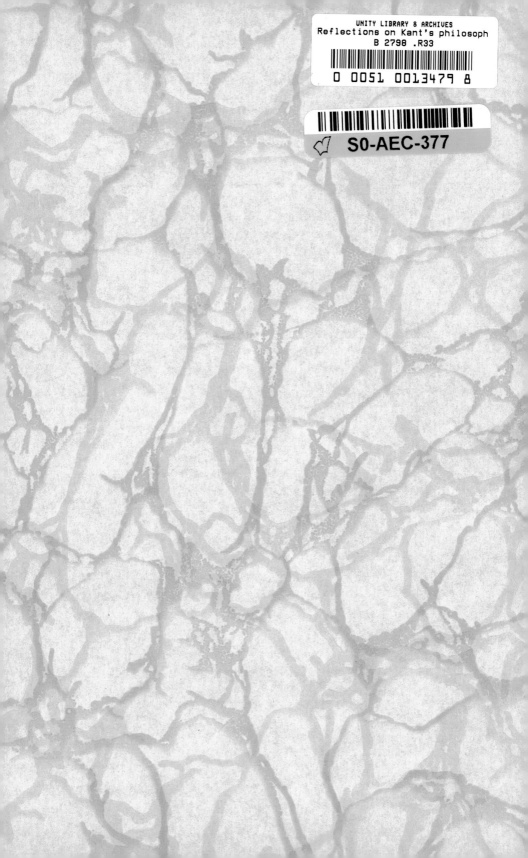

Reflections on
Kant's Philosophy

Edited by W. H. Werkmeister

A Florida State University Book

UNIVERSITY PRESSES OF FLORIDA

Gainesville

Library of Congress Cataloging in Publication Data

Main entry under title:

Reflections on Kant's philosophy.

"A Florida State University book."
Papers presented at a symposium celebrating Immanuel Kant's 250th
birthday sponsored by the Florida State University, Dept. of Philosophy,
Apr. 19-20, 1974.
Includes bibliographical references and index.
1. Kant, Immanuel, 1724-1804–Congresses. I. Werkmeister, William
Henry, 1901-   II. Florida. State University, Tallahassee. Dept. of
Philosophy.
B2798.R33   193   75-20376
ISBN 0-8130-0541-8

CONTENTS

ACKNOWLEDGEMENT

Each of the following chapters was presented as a paper at Florida State University on an occasion celebrating Immanuel Kant's 250th birthday.

Arrangements for this symposium were made possible by a generous grant from the University through Dr. Robert M. Johnson, Provost of Graduate Studies and Research, and the Graduate Research Council of the University. The Department of Philosophy gratefully acknowledges this support.

W. H. W.

THE CONTRIBUTORS

LEWIS WHITE BECK, Burbank Professor of Intellectual and Moral Philosophy at the University of Rochester, received his Ph.D. from Duke University in 1935. He has been Dean of the Graduate School at Rochester, a visiting professor at George Washington University, Columbia University, the University of Minnesota, Bryn Mawr College, the University of Western Ontario, and the Sir George Williams University. He was a Rosenwald and a Guggenheim Fellow, and is best known for his translations of Kant's *Critique of Practical Reason* and other Kantian works, and for his numerous perceptive essays on Kant's philosophy.

GERHARD FUNKE, professor of philosophy and former vice-chancellor of the University of Mainz, received his Ph.D. at the University of Bonn in 1938. He has been a visiting professor at the Sorbonne, at several Latin American universities, in Japan, India, and the USSR. He is vice-president of the Société

Européenne de Culture, president of the International Kant-Gesellschaft and editor of *Kant-Studien.* A lifetime member of the Institut Internationale de Philosophie, he is the author of twelve books and more than seventy articles in professional journals and various collections of essays.

MOLTKE S. GRAM, associate professor of philosophy at the University of Iowa, studied at the Christian Albrechts Universität (Kiel, West Germany), John Hopkins University, and the Karl Ruprecht University at Heidelberg, receiving his doctor's degree at Indiana University in 1965. He is the author of *Kant, Ontology and the A Priori* (1968) and of a number of articles on various aspects of Kant's philosophy and related topics. In 1967, he edited *Kant: Disputed Questions.*

TED B. HUMPHREY, associate professor at Arizona State University, received his Ph.D. from the University of California, San Diego. His specialty is philosophy in the seventeenth and eighteenth centuries. In this field he has published a number of articles in various philosophical journals, including the *Journal of the History of Philosophy* and the *Journal of the History of Ideas.* He has been the recipient of a special grant from Arizona State University in support of his work on Kant.

GEORGE SCHRADER, professor of philosophy and chairman of the Department of Philosophy at Yale University, was a Fulbright scholar at the University of Munich and is a member of the editorial boards of *Kant-Studien,* the *American Philosophical Quarterly,* and the *Journal for Existentialism.* He has published extensively in professional journals and has contributed to a number of collections of essays in philosophy.

FREDERICK P. VAN DE PITTE, associate professor of philosophy at the University of Alberta at Edmonton, completed his doctoral studies at the University of Southern California in 1966. He is the author of *Kant as Philosophical Anthropologist* (1971) and of a number of articles on Kant, Heidegger, Descartes, and Kierkegaard.

W. H. WERKMEISTER is professor emeritus at Florida State University where he has been on the faculty since 1966. He studied at the Universities of Münster and Frankfort, Germany, receiving his Ph.D. from the University of Nebraska in 1927. He remained at Nebraska as a member of the faculty until 1953 when he became director of the School of Philosophy at the University of Southern California. He served as director *pro tem* of the Institute for American Culture at the University of Berlin, was the first Tully Cleon Knoles Lecturer at the University of the Pacific, a visiting professor at Harvard, and special lecturer at the University of Istanbul. He is a past-president of the American Philosophical Association, of the Florida Philosophical Association, and the American Society for Value Inquiry. He is the author of ten books, including a two-volume *Historical Spectrum of Value Theories* and *Immanuel Kant: The Architectonic and Development of His Philosophy*, and of numerous articles in professional journals.

INTRODUCTION

April 22, 1974, was the 250th birthday of Immanuel Kant. The Department of Philosophy of Florida State University recognized this event by arranging a symposium on Kant's philosophy for April 19 and 20, 1974. The chapters of this book are the papers presented and discussed on that occasion. Each deals with a particular aspect of Kant's philosophy; together, they will picture for the reader many of the facets of Kant's philosophy.

It is, of course, well known that the problem of analytic and synthetic judgments—and especially of synthetic judgments a priori—is central to Kant's epistemology. But the problem was there before Kant made it a key issue of his philosophy. Professor Beck effectively shows (chapter 1) how the problem emerged in the philosophies of Locke and Hume, and found further development in Leibniz's distinction between truths of reason and truths of fact, although Kant himself does not mention these antecedents. Professor Beck also provides proof that long before Hume awoke Kant from his dogmatic slumber, Crusius had developed a theory as to how synthetic judgments are possible a priori, and Kant was certainly familiar with Crusius's work. What is of special importance, however, is Kant's response to Eberhard's contention that the problem of synthetic judgments a priori had already been solved by Christian Wolff. Against this charge Professor Beck shows wherein consists the originality of Kant's thesis, and how Kant would answer his modern critics, most of whom have merely repeated Eberhard's criticism.

The theory of the so-called "double affection" has been suggested by commentators on Kant's Critical Philosophy as a possible escape from glaring inconsistencies allegedly found in Kant's *Critique of Pure Reason.* In his penetrating analysis of the problem at issue Moltke Gram not only provides a clear and comprehensive statement of what is at issue; he also examines critically the evidence submitted in support of the thesis. He discusses specifically the nature of the problem for which the thesis of the "double affection" is presumed to be a solution. According to that thesis, Kant provides two kinds of objects which affect the subject: There are things in themselves which affect the self; and there are appearances in themselves which act on our sensibility and are independent of whatever characteristics attach to our sensory receptors. However, in compelling arguments Professor Gram shows that, no matter how the thesis of the "double affection" is formulated and developed, Kant's distinctions between "appearances and appearances in themselves, appearances and appearances of appearances, and appearances and things in themselves neither imply a double affection nor require the distinction between two kinds of affection," and that Kant's distinction between subjectivity and ideality does also not require a double affection. But only Professor Gram's fully developed argument can show how and why the thesis of the "double affection" fails both exegetically and philosophically, and how the dilemma originally facing Kant's theory disappears.

Thus the first two chapters of this book deal with problems related to Kant's epistemological position; the next two take up special problems related to his moral philosophy.

Professor Schrader's basic theme is that ethical theory must not only justify norms of moral conduct, it must also give us a sound description of man as a moral agent; and that man's freedom must be shown to be a fact rather than a mere possibility. What is needed, therefore, is a theory of human nature that will effectively integrate the empirical and the moral components in man's existence. Seen in this perspective, Kant's "metaphysics of morals" is essentially "a metaphysics of human existence." This implies that to the "transcendental unity of apperception" (of the first *Critique*) there corresponds a "transcendental unity of volition," and it is this fact which provides a solid basis of normative ethics. Kant, however, not only failed to develop this idea but, so Professor Schrader shows, accepted assumptions about empirical motivation which are open to serious question. The problem of Kant's ethics is "to show how reason can regulate the empirical will"; but is his solution of this problem fully consistent with his anthropological theory? In a well-developed and sustained argument Schrader shows that it is crucially important for Kant's analysis that the moral maxim not be confused with the intention of a natural inclination; and on this point Kant is apparently not sufficiently rigorous in his interpretation. Several difficulties arise when, on Kantian grounds, we try to relate moral volition to impulse and inclination. Professor Schrader discusses them in detail, suggesting that we must assess them "from the perspective of the agent rather than an observer," and that the whole problem of sociability must also be taken into consideration; for it is impossible for a sociable disposition to be developed without maxims which serve to provide it with intentional meaning. Kant's basic error, so Schrader finds, stems from his conviction that ethics can be based on the pure concept of duty and, therefore, on the concept of a pure rational will. That is to say, error arises, not from a confusion of descriptive and normative analysis (as Moore alleged), but from an incomplete descriptive analysis of what it means to exist as a moral agent in our everyday world. Kant has given us a basic perspective but not the whole story.

While Professor Schrader gives us a new perspective on the basis of Kant's ethics, Professor Funke projects problems of ethics into the field of politics and the meaning of human history. The key idea here is Kant's thesis that nature intended man to "develop completely on his own everything which goes beyond the [mere] mechanical regulation of his animal being." This being so, the problem centers around the actualization of this idea in history; and the question now is: How is man's freedom to realize his ultimate destiny possible in a world in which causal laws prevail? Kant deals with the problem in *Idea for a Universal History from a Cosmopolitan Point of View.* Professor Funke carefully and critically analyzes the argument of the treatise, coming to the conclusion that "necessity and reason bring man to the realization that national law, international law, and international civil law are indispensable" to the full realization of all human potentialities. Entailed in this is the demand for an arrangement of international relations that will ensure the actualization of "eternal peace." To give concrete content to his argument Professor Funke examines Kant's specific "Articles of Peace," arguing (with Kant) that "a universal state of world citizenship may be brought about only at some future time" as mankind gradually prepares itself for it. In this process, as far as Kant is concerned, the moral law must be kept holy and, for each individual and for mankind as a whole, eternal peace becomes a moral task—the ultimate realization of practical reason in action.

In my own paper, "Kant's Philosophy and Modern Physics," I start with the generally held view that, in the development of his epistemology, Kant stood firmly committed to the principles of Newtonian mechanics; that, in fact, in the "Analogies of Experience" he provides an axiomatized basis for an interpretation of nature for which Newtonian mechanics served as a model; and that his "Principle of Causality" is in effect but a generalization of Newton's First Law of Motion. I show, however, that there are aspects of Kant's interpretation of physical reality that go far beyond Newtonian mechanics in the direction of modern science. I show, for example, that Kant's "Principle of Causality" is perfectly reconcilable with Heisenberg's "Principle of Uncertainty." But I also show that Kant's conception of reason as a cognitive faculty aiming at the subordination of all facts of nature to one single Principle is at least a parallel to the modern projection of a unified field theory in physics. I then argue that in the first and second Antinomies Kant points up problems that have their counterparts in modern physics. Does the world have a beginning, or does it not have a beginning? I see here the "big bang theory" versus the "steady state theory" of modern cosmology. More significant, however, is Kant's conception of a general theory of relativity which goes far beyond Newtonian mechanics and approaches (even in the supporting arguments) Einstein's general theory. Furthermore, I present indisputable evidence that Kant abandoned Newtonian atoms in favor of the conception of undulatory and vibrating motions in an "ether" which is but hypostatized space itself. This, I submit, is not far removed from the basic conception of matter characteristic of modern wave mechanics. Only the mathematical formulations are lacking. My final point is that in his interpretation of living organisms Kant avoids both a mechanistic and a vitalistic interpretation. When he argues that "an organic body is a machine which creates itself as to form," he states almost verbatim the conclusion which Jacques Monod (Nobel Prize winner in physiology and medicine) stated in 1970: "L'organisme est une machine qui se construit elle-même."

Professor Van De Pitte raises the question: What would be the effect on Kant's Critical Philosophy if the principle of reflective judgment (pertaining, as it does, to problems of teleology) were given the status of a constitutive principle instead of being regarded as a regulative principle of merely subjective validity? In writing his third *Critique* Kant aimed at bringing nature and morality into a coherent system, revealing that the world we live in is a whole within which purposes can be realized through freedom. Such interpretation, however, is possible only if design is a constituent element of the natural order, complementing mechanical causality. But if purposiveness is given a constituent role along with mechanical causality, this entails a shift in the merely regulative role of the ideas of reason. A teleological proof for the existence of God would then be possible but morality would be reduced to an externally imposed authoritarianism. However, Professor Van De Pitte argues that there might be an alternative, namely, to conceive purposiveness not as a category but as a pure form, along with space and time, through which the imagination expresses its inherently teleological operation. Admittedly, this revision of Kant's epistemology would be clearly heretical; but it would involve no violation of Kant's own procedural norms—as Professor Van De Pitte procedes to show. In fact, the revision would provide Kant with an absolute answer to Hume and, at the same time, would make his philosophy surprisingly compatible with contemporary scientific knowledge.

Professor Humphrey's topic is a critical examination of Kant's assertion that "reason has insight only into that which it creates in accordance with its own plan." In order to clarify Kant's meaning, he examines in detail the argument of the

Preface (*Vorrede;* Kemp-Smith's translation: Introduction) to the first *Critique* in which Kant discusses the problem of necessity and certainty, using logic, mathematics and natural science as paradigm cases of scientific knowledge. Although his interpretation of logic depends upon a distinction between genetic apriority and logical apriority, Kant himself does not make this distinction (at least not explicitly) but presupposes it in his characterization of logic as a disposition to organize objects of consciousness, be they pure or empirical. No "revolution" was necessary to make logic scientific. It is different, so Humphrey argues, with geometry and with mathematics in general. Here the turn to science did require a "Revolution der Denkart" through which an a priori element is introduced into geometrical knowledge. The development of natural science Kant saw in a similar way as the result of spontaneous reflection on nature in hypotheses and experimentation. His problem now was: Can this method of science be applied in the field of metaphysics? To do so requires a "revolution in method" which replaces traditional speculative metaphysics with a new critical metaphysics; and this requires a new epistemology. The crucial point is that we must distinguish between things as appearances and things-in-themselves. The first half of the *Critique of Pure Reason* explicates this idea, proving indirectly the truth of Kant's Copernican Revolution. In part 2 of this chapter, Professor Humphrey examines the adequacy of Kant's new approach and finds that, as far as Kant is concerned, two quite different kinds of a priori elements are involved in geometry, and that because of this fact various problems arise for Kant. Humphrey deals with them in detail, coming to the conclusion that Kant's Copernican Revolution has failed in at least one respect: It does not yield certainty concerning metric space. A reader of Professor Humphrey's paper would miss a great deal of his argument if he were not to take into consideration its development in the Notes.

All in all, the reflections upon Kant's philosophy here presented are challenging and illuminating. Old problems are seen in new perspectives, and new problems are raised for the first time. The discussions are in themselves proof that much can yet be learned from a close study of Kant's philosophy taken as a whole.

ANALYTIC AND SYNTHETIC JUDGMENTS BEFORE KANT

Lewis White Beck

"Men who never think independently have nevertheless the acuteness to discover everything, after it has
been once shown them, in what was said long since,
though no one was ever able to see it there before."

Prolegomena § 3

"Es ist auch schon das gewöhnliche Schicksal alles
Neuen in Wissenschaften, wenn man ihm nichts ent-
gegensetzen kann, dass man es doch wenigstens als
längst bekannt bei Aelteren antreffe."

*—Ueber eine Entdeckung nach der alle neue Kri-
tik der reinen Vernunft durch eine ältere ent-
behrlich gemacht werden soll* (AA 8, 242)

It is perhaps customary in introductory courses in the history of
philosophy, and it is not unknown in the literature—including
some of my own writings—to introduce Kant's distinction between analytic and synthetic judgments by referring to Leibni-
z's distinction between truths of reason and truths of fact and

to Hume's distinction between relations of ideas and matters of fact. Some, more venturesome perhaps, seek the origin of the distinction in Locke's dichotomy of trifling and instructive propositions, in Hobbes' of truths of universal propositions and truths of existential propositions and even farther back in truths dependent upon the intellect of God and thus dependent upon the will of God.

Under the common assumption that pre-Kantian philosophers equated whatever in their terminology is said to be equivalent to "analytic" with a priori and whatever in their terminology is said to be equivalent to "synthetic" with a posteriori, the following summary table is not uncommon:

	a priori	*a posteriori*
analytic	relations of ideas truths of reason	none
synthetic	none	matters of fact truths of fact

1

The schema just presented is not exactly wrong, but it is woefully incomplete. It was the thesis of a famous paper by Arthur O. Lovejoy[1] that the table was so incomplete and wrong that it created the fiction that Kant had something original to contribute besides a new terminology, and that if the contribution of one other philosopher (Wolff) is put into the table, it will turn out that Kant was either a mere plagiarist or else unpardonably ignorant of the state of the problem.

Indeed one of the most remarkable things, which ought first to strike the eye, is that Kant *seems to have been ignorant of the information summarized in the table.* For he says, "Perhaps even the distinction between analytic and synthetic judgments has never previously been considered,"[2] and, more specifically, "the dogmatic philosophers Wolff and his acute follower Baumgarten altogether neglected this apparently obvious distinction."[3]

Yet in the same paragraph in the *Prolegomena* he says he finds "an indication of the division" in Locke's *Essay,* Book IV, chapter 3, § § 9-10, where Locke draws a distinction between our certainty of identity and diversity (Kant says "identity or contradiction"—a significant slip) and that of coexistence, of which we have little a priori knowledge. But he seems to have overlooked a more obvious source, namely, Book IV, chapters 7 and 8, of the *Essay,* where Locke distinguishes between "a real truth [which] conveys with it instructive real knowledge" by stating "a necessary consequence of a precise complex idea . . . not contained in it," and "trifling propositions" which are either mere identities or affirmations "when any part of a complex idea is predicated of the whole."[4] Thus it seems that Locke had not only distinguished between analytic and synthetic judgments but that he had held, and that Kant knew that he had held, that some of the latter could be known with certainty, that is, that they were a priori.

In the same paragraph, Kant says that Locke was so vague and indefinite in his remarks on a priori synthetic knowledge that he did not stimulate even Hume "to make investigations concerning this sort of propositions." Yet again and again Kant writes as if Hume had distinguished between analytic and synthetic judgments and had categorically denied the possibility of a priori synthetic judgments. He did so, Kant held, because he failed to draw a needed distinction between the synthetic judgments of the understanding, which may be known a priori for objects of possible experience, and those of reason, which profess to be about things which can never be met with in experience. Since Hume agreed with Kant that the latter type of synthetic a priori knowledge is impossible, his failure to make the needed distinction led him to reject the possibility of any synthetic judgments (or possible experience) known a priori, while Kant, precisely by making this distinction, did not have to condemn all a priori synthetic judgments but only those which claim to refer beyond experience.[5]

Hence Hume concluded, according to Kant, that all *genuine* a priori knowledge must be analytic. Concerning the judgments which are commonly believed to be a priori but not analytic (namely, the causal maxim), Hume went on to give a psychological explanation of the illusion that they are a priori. Since Kant had such insights into Hume's mode of argument, I cannot explain why he did not cite the opening paragraphs of section 4 of the *Enquiry,* a passage known to every schoolboy. Here Hume draws his famous distinction between relations of ideas and matters of fact. Kant must have read there: "The contrary of every matter of fact is still possible because it can never imply a contradiction and is conceived by the mind with the same facility and distinctness as if ever so conformable to reality." In the *Enquiry,* therefore, matter of fact judgments meet one of the criteria of syntheticity. Accordingly, relations of ideas "discoverable by the mere operation of thought without dependence on what is anywhere existent in the universe" seem to be judged in what Kant called analytic judgments.

Yet had Kant read the *Treatise* he would have discovered that perhaps Hume did not mean exactly what he seemed to be saying; and if we, who can read the *Treatise,* do so, we perhaps find out why Kant was correct in not taking this to mean that relations of ideas, even if (presumably) testable by contradiction, are equivalent to the relation expressed in an analytical judgment. The relations of ideas in the *Enquiry* correspond to the "necessary and unalterable" philosophical relations of the *Treatise,* relations "which depend entirely on the ideas which we compare together."[6] But the necessary and unalterable philosophical relations are not analytical in the sense that one of the relata is included in the other, nor in the sense that the denial of such a relation involves a formal contradiction.[7]

By "contradiction" Hume did not mean merely an assertion like "A is not A." He means also "A is not B" where an A that is not a B is "inconceivable" or "unimaginable."

> Wherein consists the difference betwixt believing and disbelieving any propositions, that are prov'd by intuition or demonstration. In that case, the person, who assents, not only conceives the ideas according to the proposition, but is necessarily determin'd to conceive them in that particular manner, either immediately or by the imposition of other ideas. Whatever is absurd is unintelligible; nor is it possible for

the imagination to conceive anything contrary to a demonstration.[8]

Thus even before Kant there were ambiguities which have recently been brought to light again in the continuing debate about the criterion of analyticity, though of course Hume is more ambiguous than those whom Quine is criticizing. For Hume did not mean by "contradiction" a formal contradiction alone; "inconceivability" means not merely logical nonsense, but also unimaginability, and even counter-intuitivity. His relations of ideas are not trifling propositions and not, therefore, analytical propositions as Kant understood the term, though this cannot be seen by anyone who, like Kant, reads only the *Enquiry* and not also the *Treatise.* Had Kant read Hume's *Treatise,* he would have found Hume tacitly admitting a class of intuitively and demonstratively necessary relations of ideas which are not testable by the logical law of contradiction.

Hume differed from Locke in holding that the causal relation is neither intuitively nor demonstratively known. Hence he concluded that it is a matter-of-fact relation which can be known, if at all, only a posteriori. It was this inference which awoke Kant from his dogmatic slumber. He "generalized Hume's problem" and saw that if the syntheticity of the causal maxim implied its aposteriority, then all the propositions even of mathematics (as well as metaphysics) can be known only a posteriori. He held that Hume himself had been saved from the absurdity of holding mathematics to be a posteriori only because he had made the mistake of holding its judgments to be analytic.[9] Believing as Kant did that mathematical judgments were both synthetic and a priori, he had to investigate how it is possible for there to be such judgments, and he "solemnly and legally suspended" all metaphysicians from their occupation until they had answered the question of how this was possible.[10]

2

Leibniz's distinction between truths of reason and truths of fact is another obvious source of Kant's distinction which he does not anywhere mention. Its *locus classicus* is the *Monadology:*

31. Our reasonings are grounded on two great principles, that of contradiction, in virtue of which we judge false that which involves a contradiction, and true that which is opposed or contradictory to the false.

33. There are also two kinds of truths, those of reason and those of fact. Truths of reason are necessary and their opposite is impossible. When a truth is necessary, its reason can be found by analysis, resolving it into more simple ideas and truths, until we come to those that are primary.

35. There are simple ideas, of which no definition can be given; there are also axioms and postulates, in a word, primary principles; and these are identical propositions whose opposite involves an express contradiction.

From these well-known passages it is inferred that truths of fact are synthetic and truths of reason are analytic, and that only the latter can be known a priori. But we must remember that the *Monadology* was a book for popular consumption, and the esoteric doctrine of Leibniz, which we know mostly through his unpublished writings, is very much more complicated.

According to the esoteric doctrine, in all true affirmative propositions the concept of the predicate is included in the concept of the subject.[11] Therefore all true affirmative propositions are identities or partial identities (that is, analytic propositions), and all false affirmative propositions are self-contradictory. If the demonstration of the proposition by reduction to an identity through substitution of definientia for definienda can be accomplished in a finite number of steps, the judgment is called an explicit identity even though its form is not "A is A" but rather "A.B is B" or "A is A.B." If the reduction cannot be effected in a finite number of steps, the proposition is only a virtual identity and cannot be known by showing the self-contradictoriness of its contradictory; though intrinsically analytic, it is known to us in other ways than an expressly analytic judgment.[12]

The *Monadology* gives a succinct account of how we know a theorem in geometry, without taking these esoteric complications into account: by substituting definientia we come to axioms, and axioms are explicit identities whose "opposites involve an express contradiction." Earlier (1678) in a letter to Conring Leibniz had written:

> Demonstration is a chain of definitions. . . . All truths can be resolved into definitions, identical propositions, and observations—though purely intelligible truths do not need observations.[13]

But there are two places where this program breaks down, at least one of which Leibniz himself admitted.

(1) There must be *primae veritates* which are unprovable and therefore not analytic, because explicit identity or contradiction cannot obtain between simple unanalyzable terms. The contradictory of a *prima veritas* cannot, in spite of *Monadology* § 35, be self-contradictory. In Russell's words: "Any relation between simple ideas is necessarily synthetic. For the analytic relation . . . can only hold between ideas of which one at least is complex."[14]

In a work unknown to his contemporaries but known to Kant, Leibniz seems to have seen this difficulty. He substituted "comparison or concurrence *(concours)*" for the stricter "identity and and contradiction" between simple ideas.[15] He furthermore distinguished primitive truths known by intuition into two kinds: primitive truths of reason and primitive truths of fact.

Under primitive truths of reason he listed "identical affirmatives," which are trifling, and "identical negatives," which are either under the law of contradiction or are "disparates." "Disparates" are propositions that state that the object of one idea is not the object of another idea, as "that heat is not the same thing as color." Disparates "may be asserted independently of all proof or of reduction to opposition or to the principle of contradiction."[16]

(2) A like problem is met with not merely at the end of a reduction to identity, but along the course of the reduction from an apparently synthetic judgment to an identity. Definition must be by analyzing complex concepts and then demonstrating the identity of the analysantia. In order to give real definitions (merely nominal definitions trivialize the project[17]), we must be able to show the compossibility and necessary

coherence of predicates in a complex concept. If these predicates are simple (conceived per se) it cannot be demonstrated that they must co-inhere in one subject concept by appealing to the law of contradiction, because there is no formal contradiction in the conjunction of two simple predicates.

As Russell says, "This compatibility, since it is presupposed by the analytic judgment, cannot itself be analytic;[18] and Leibniz himself says:

> As often as I combine several things which are not conceived through themselves, experience is needed, not only of the fact that they are conceived by me at the same time in the same subject . . . but also of the fact that they really exist in the same subject.[19]

(Perhaps by "experience" Leibniz here means to include intuition and not merely empirical observation, which he excluded in his letter to Conring cited above.)

From all this it follows that while Leibniz had, in his *exoteric* works, a reasonably clear distinction between analytic and synthetic judgments, he was not able to maintain in his *esoteric* works that all a priori judgments are analytic. It may well be that Kant was thinking of Leibniz when he wrote:

> As it was found that the conclusions of mathematicians all proceed according to the law of contradiction . . . men persuaded themselves that the fundamental principles were known by the same law. This was a great mistake, for a synthetical proposition can indeed be established by the law of contradiction but only by presupposing another synthetical proposition from which it follows, but never by that law alone.[20]

3

Wolff had an easier task than Leibniz because he did not adhere to Leibniz's analytical theory of judgment according to which *praedicatum inest subiecto.*[21] For him, judgment is the *Verknüpfung* or *Trennung* of two concepts.[22] With this definition he inquired into the ground of the connection or separation of the concepts and found it in the subject as the *Bedingung* of the predicate (*Aussage*) according to the principle of sufficient reason. But the latter principle was for him a logical principle, demonstrable by the law of contradiction; and hence Wolff did not adequately distinguish between the way in which a subject implies a predicate in what we call an analytical proposition and the way in which it is a mere condition in what we call a synthetic judgment.[23] Thus he did not emphasize the difference between identities and other necessary propositions connecting simple ideas, which ought to have kept him from holding that the denials of the latter are self-contradictory as are the denials of the former.[24] He recognizes that the connection of two simple ideas is not "thought through identity" because they do not determine one another, but *"fieri posse constant (sive vi experientiae, sive demonstrationis) combinari posse intelliguntur"*[25] and this *combinari posse* can be seen by *ratio intuitiva.* A concept is *gedenkbar* if one can see the agreement *(consensio, convenientia)* of the components. But he falls back into the old way of thinking when he holds that the *ungedenkbare* combinations are self-contradictory.[26] This is certainly how Kant read him: "The only conflict they [the Leibniz-Wolffians] recognize is that of contradiction."[27] Because he placed so much more emphasis on the self-contradictoriness of the contradictory than on the intuition of the *consensio,* he was vulnerable to attack from men like Crusius, as we shall see.

We turn now to Wolff's theory of the constitution of complex subjects *(notiones foecundae*[28]*).* With such a subject, the criterion of the self-contradictoriness of the contradictory of a judgment is more apt. For now he is considering truly analytical judgments; but the whole burden of proof is shifted from synthetic *judgments* to synthetic *subjects.* Lambert criticized him for this, saying that he took nominal definitions "as it were gratis" and "without noticing it, hid all the difficulties in them."[29] This, however, is unfair to Wolff, for he devoted much effort to establishing the real possibility (not merely the logical possibility) of complex concepts.[30] Regrettably, however, Wolff (perhaps not clearly seeing the importance of the distinction) does not give in any systematic order the criteria by which the real possibility of a concept is to be decided, that is, by which the possibility of the co-inherence of independent *essentialia*[31] is to be established. But he does, in various places in the *Ontologia,* provide several conditions. One—*"ab existentia ad possibilitatem valet consequentia"*[32] —is a posteriori, four (or five) others are apparently a priori. A concept consisting of the *notae* A and B is a priori possible if A and B presuppose one another or if one follows from the other by demonstration.[33] (For these, presumably, the law of contradiction suffices.) Another test is the constructability of the concept.[34] This is, at least verbally, an anticipation of the test for the possibility of mathematical concepts in Kant. But Wolff does not expand on this and probably did not see the significance of what he had said, since he regarded the syllogism, not construction, as the paradigm of mathematical proof.[35] Finally there is the *"combinari posse intelliguntur"* to which I have already alluded. The last, and perhaps the next to last, are the only ones which can build synthetic real concepts a priori. The ones about demonstrability are obviously inadequate for the addition of independent predicates, and the first one does so only a posteriori.

In summary, then, Wolff admits two kinds of propositions whose contradictories he holds to be self-contradictory:

(i) Empty sentences *propositio identica,* ("A is A"), sometimes[36] called axioms.

(ii) Judgments *per essentialia, modus praedicandi essentialia,*[37] ("A is B" where A is a complex concept in which B is an *essentia*), elsewhere called axioms[38] and identities.[39]

Lovejoy[40] calls (ii) synthetical judgments a priori because they have a synthetical or "fecund" subject, but they are clearly analytical by Kant's criterion.

To these must be added a third type of judgment, some of which can be known a priori and others a posteriori:

(iii) Judgments *per attributum, modus praedicandi attributa*[41], ("A is C" where C is an attribute of A not included in its definition or essence but having its sufficient reason in the essence.)

Since it is judgments of this kind that were claimed later, by Eberhard, to be synthetic and known a priori, we might wish that Wolff had given a systematic treatment of them in some one place. His examples, however, are instructive.

(a) His first example is meant to be a judgment known a priori: "It is an attribute of a triangle *(Dreyeck)* that it has three angles *(Winkel)*. For this is attributed to it *(komment ihm zu)* because a triangle is a space enclosed in three lines."[42] Presumably this is a logical "because," since the proposition is supposed to be reducible to axioms and definitions which are identities;[43] but elsewhere he says it is evident "by construction."[44]

(b) "Hardness is an attribute of stone but not of wax" is obviously a posteriori, and Wolff tells us how to find out by experience which predicates are attributes and which are mere accidents of things.[45]

(c) Finally, there are judgments which can be known a priori in the sense that, as Kant says, they cannot "be derived immediately from experience but from a universal rule"; but they are not a priori ("completely a priori," as Kant says) in the sense that they can be known completely independently of all experience, since the "universal rule" is itself based upon experience.[46] Wolff holds that one can "prove" a judgment *per attributum* by syllogism. His example is "Wood can be cut."[47] The proof is given by providing a definition of cutting ("the separation of parts") and of wood ("made up of fibers"). Such a proof converts "historical" (that is, empirical) knowledge into "philosophical" knowledge or "knowledge of the reason of things."[48]

4

Crusius, the principal pre-Kantian critic of Wolff, is now largely forgotten, but Kant himself did not forget him. Long before Hume awoke Kant from his dogmatic slumber, Crusius[49] had already pointed out what Kant was later to relearn from Hume at a critical point in his own development when the impact of Hume's discovery about causality "gave quite a new direction to [Kant's] investigations."[50]

J. S. Beck[51] in 1793 wrote Kant that Crusius's *Weg zur Gewissheit* (1747) provided a better "indication" of the analytic-synthetic distinction than the passages Kant had cited from Locke, but Kant knew Crusius's work already in the 1760s. In his *Dissertatio de uso et limitibus principii rationis determinantis, vulgo sufficientis* (1743) Crusius had criticized Wolff's attempted derivation[52] of the principle of sufficient reason from the principle of contradiction. In his *Entwurf der nothwendigen Vernunftwahrheiten* (1745) and *Weg zur Gewissheit* he had criticized Wolff for believing in the sufficiency of the principle of contradiction for the establishment and testing of a priori truth. "The question," he says, "is not whether, upon presupposing [certain] concepts we are required by the law of contradiction to deny the opposite; this is well known. The question is: whether the law of contradiction was, or even could have been, the sufficient reason for the constitution *(Einrichtung)* of the concepts themselves."[53] He answers this question in the negative.

He takes the case of causality.[54] "Every effect has a cause" is clear from the principle of contradiction, but that does not show that the existence of one thing is dependent on that of another. The latter can be denied without contradiction, because the subjects to which existence is attributed are different and exist at different times. Experience, even Wolff saw, must be called upon to discover what *specific* thing is the cause of another; but unlike Wolff, Crusius believed that the general principle cannot be established merely by a proof from the law of contradiction. That is to say, in Kantian language, Crusius sought a proof of the principle of causality as, or as derived from, a synthetic a priori principle. Real knowledge must be founded on a different principle from the law of contradiction, which suffices for what Crusius calls "hypothetical knowledge."

We have seen earlier philosophers supplement demonstration with intuition so as to have two bases for certain knowledge. Hume denied that the causal principle is known in either way, and therefore asserted that it is not known a priori. Crusius, on the contrary, supplements demonstrative knowledge with two *Vernunftwahrheiten* which he calls the "principles of inseparability and uncombinability": "Whatever two things cannot be thought apart from one another cannot exist or be possible apart from one another," and "Whatever two things cannot be thought with and beside one another cannot be possible or exist with and beside one another."[55] These give the ground why contradictories cannot coexist or be compossible, but they go far beyond the realm of the merely logically impossible. The real ground of a predicate or a relation must be distinguished from the logical ground, and the connection of real ground with the predicate can be known a priori; but the real ground itself can be known only through experience.

Not only did Crusius have a clear conception of the difference between analytic and synthetic judgments; he also had a theory as to how synthetic judgments are possible a priori. It was not a theory that Kant could accept, as he accepted the consequences of Crusius's distinction between judgments from logical grounds and judgments from real grounds. After a long period in which he honored Crusius for drawing the right distinction he turned against him for failing to show how synthetic judgments can be known a priori: Crusius, he said, made mere custom and incapacity to think otherwise into an objective necessity, and could get to objective necessity only by accepting a preestablished harmony between innate ideas and their objects.[56] But what Kant did learn from Crusius must not be underestimated; he learned that "the rain never follows the wind because of the law of identity."[57]

5

I shall not attempt to recount the steps by which Kant was led to make his classical distinction between synthetic and analytic judgments. I refrain from this for two reasons: first, we do not actually know what they were or when they were taken; and second, what is known about them has already been adequately presented.[58] Rather than going through this history of the development of the distinction, I wish rather to turn to a defense of the originality of his distinction which Kant made late in his life: *On a Discovery according to which the whole new Critique of Pure Reason is Rendered Unnecessary by an Earlier One*, published in 1790 against Eberhard.[59] This is an important paper both historically and philosophically—historically because it is Kant's *Auseinandersetzung* with the Wolffian tradition; philosophically, because it shows us how Kant would answer his modern critics who deny that there are synthetic judgments known a priori—for most modern critics have, perhaps unbeknownst to themselves, merely repeated Eberhard's criticisms.[60]

At the end of section 3 above, I gave Wolff's division of judgments which are not formal identities into judgments *per essentialia* and judgments *per attributum*. Eberhard holds that they are both a priori, and that whatever is valid in Kant's distinction between analytic and synthetic judgments a priori coincides with Wolff's distinction. Eberhard calls judgments *per attributum* synthetic because they affirm attributes which are not included in the essence of the subject concept, and a priori because they have their sufficient ground in the subject concept from which they may be explicated by analysis. Hence Eberhard holds that the problem to which the *Critique of Pure Reason* is addressed—namely, "How are synthetic judgments a priori possible?"—had already been answered by Wolff, and that all Kant contributed was a new (and confusing) terminology. Against the accusation that the distinction was already known and was not invented by Kant, Kant replied:

> Maybe so! But the reason why the importance of the distinction has not been recognized seems to be that all a priori judgments were regarded [by Wolff] as analytic ... so the whole point of the distinction disappeared.[61]

In modern terminology (which we owe to C. I. Lewis)[62] "synthetic judgments a priori" are sometimes said to be implicitly analytic judgments—ampliative ("synthetic") by the criterion of "what is actually thought in the subject concept, though not so distinctly and with the same (full) consciousness,"[63] but explicative ("analytic") by the criterion of logical deducibility and testability by the law of contradiction.

Kant and Eberhard agree—Kant accusingly, Eberhard proudly[64]—that the distinction between essence and attribute which underlies Eberhard's analytic-synthetic distinction is one drawn in general logic. But, Kant says, "The explanation of the possibility of synthetic judgments is a problem with which general logic has nothing to do. It need not even so much as know the problem by name."[65] In short, the problem as Kant sees it is one of epistemology, or what he calls transcendental logic; hence he feels justified in classifying judgments according to their *grounds (Wahrheitsgründe)*[66] and not merely as they are classified in formal logic *(per essentialia, per attributum).*

The essence with which Eberhard is concerned consists of those marks *(notae)* that are the necessary and sufficient conditions for the definition of the concept. The attributes for Eberhard are those marks that logically follow from the concept of the subject ("belong to it") but are not explicitly included in the logical essence or its definiens ("do not lie in it").[6][7] We can be sure that a predicate signifies an attribute if it is a logical consequence of the essence or definition, so that its denial would be self-contradictory. Thus "having more than two sides" is an attribute of a triangle, since "having three sides," the essence of triangle, logically entails "having more than two sides." An attribute which follows analytically from the definition or logical essence by the law of contradiction, as this one does, is called by Kant an "analytical predicate." Even though the judgment containing such a predicate may be ampliative or instructive for someone who does not know the implications of the defintion, Kant is now content to call a judgment analytical if it contains an analytical predicate.[6][8]

But Kant holds that there is another kind of essence which he calls "real" instead of "logical," and another kind of attribute,[6][9] which he calls "synthetic" instead of "analytic."

A synthetic attribute, a *Bestimmung*,[7][0] is one which does not follow from the logical essence and yet has a sufficient ground in the real essence.[7][1] Hence it can be necessarily predicated of the subject in a synthetic judgment. Such a judgment is a priori synthetic. (To cite Kant's own example, that space has three dimensions is not known by analysis of the definition of space [its logical essence] and yet can be known a priori to be true of space.)

The problem of the *Critique of Pure Reason* is to see how an attribute can be attached synthetically, yet a priori, to an object whose concept does not logically entail it by containing it implicitly.

A concept is logically possible if it does not entail contradictory predicates. But a logically possible concept may be without an object and thus only an *ens rationis*.[7][2] To be shown to be really and not merely logically possible, the concept must be of an object which "agrees with the formal conditions of experience"[7][3] (First Postulate of Empirical Thought), and this includes the condition of sensible intuitability.

If the sensible intuition is empirical, that is, a real perception, the concept of the perceived object is really possible because whatever is actual is possible. A judgment founded on a perception is synthetic, but a posteriori.

Sensible intutition, whether pure or empirical, cannot reveal the ontologically real essence of a thing, which is even more hidden from Kant than it was from Locke. But if the sensible intuition is pure, it reveals the real essence[74] of the thing since it is an intuition of the condition under which alone a thing can be an object for us. Though Kant calls it the real essence, to avoid confusion between what, for Kant, is known a priori and what, for him and Locke, is not known at all, let us call it the *phenomenal essence.* It consists of all the conditions of an object that are necessary if it is possible for us to experience it.

What follows from the phenomenal essence is a synthetic attribute because it is not contained in, or found by the analysis of, the logical essence. The synthetic attribute follows from the sole condition under which the object can be known, not from its metaphysical (supersensible) real essence. By virtue of the necessity with which the synthetic attribute follows from the phenomenal essence, the judgment containing this attribute is known a priori. Because it does not follow by the law of contradiction from the logical essence, it is synthetic. Hence a judgment whose predicate signifies an attribute of the phenomenal essence is a synthetic a priori judgment.

Kant's answer to Eberhard is that judgments may therefore have attributes as predicates without this fact determining whether the judgment is analytic or synthetic, a priori or a posteriori. But:

(a) If the predicate signifies an attribute or property of the logical essence, the judgment is analytic and is known a priori.

(b) If the predicate signifies a property or accident learned by experience of an object, the judgment is synthetic, but is known a posteriori.[75]

(c) If the predicate signifies an attribute or property of the phenomenal essence as the condition of intuitability, the judgment is synthetic (because the predicate does not follow from the logical essence) and known a priori (because it can be known to apply without appeal to actual experience).

NOTES

1. Lovejoy, "Kant's Antithesis of Dogmatism and Criticism," *Mind,* 1906; reprinted in M. S. Gram, ed., *Kant: Disputed Questions* (Chicago, 1967), pp. 105-30. I have examined Lovejoy's paper in considerable detail in "Lovejoy as a Critic of Kant," *Journal of the History of Ideas* 30 (1972): 471-84.
2. *K.d.r.V.* B19; not in A.
3. *Prolegomena* §3.
4. *Essay* IV, 8 §§8 and 4. In §3 explicit tautologies are counted among trifling propositions; Kant ("Fortschritte der Metaphysik," AA 20, 322) denies that they are analytical: they do not analyze and explicate. He thus distinguishes between judgments based on identity and identical judgments. Only the former are analytical.
5. *K.d.r.V.* A764-765/B792-793.
6. This correspondence has been established, to my satisfaction, by Donald W. Gotterbarn, "Hume's Theory of Relations" (Ph.D. diss. University of Rochester, 1971).
7. Gotterbarn, "Hume's Theory," pp. 92ff; W. A. Suchting, "Hume and Necessary Truth," *Dialogue* (1966–67): 47-60; R. F. Atkinson, "Hume on Mathematics," *Philosophical Quarterly* 10 (1960): 127-37.
8. *Treatise*, ed. Selby Bigge, p. 95.
9. *Critique of Practical Reason,* Preface, 3d paragraph from end.
10. *Prolegomena,* AA 5, p. 277; trans. Beck, p. 25.
11. Leibniz usually writes that the predicate is included in the subject, but sometimes that the concept of the predicate is included in (or involved in) the subject concept (*Philosophical Papers and Letters* [trans. Loemker] p. 363; cf. G. H. R. Parkinson, *Logic and Reality in Leibniz's Metaphysics* [Oxford, 1965] pp. 9, 28). Presumably he did not notice the difference, but it permitted him to believe (or shows that he did believe), in Kant's words, "that he could obtain knowledge of the inner nature of things by comparing all objects of its thought" (*K.d.r.V.* A270/B326). This was, for Kant, "the fundamental mistake of Leibniz" from which the monadology followed (H. J. Paton, "Kant on the Errors of Leibniz," in *Kant Studies Today* [ed. Beck; Lasalle,

1968, pp. 72-87] at p. 75). That the two expressions are not meant by Leibniz to be the same, and that he held to the former and not the latter, see W. E. Abraham, "Complete Concepts and Leibniz's Distinction Between Necessary and Contingent Truths," *Studia Leibnitiana* 1 (1969): 263-79.

12. But Leibniz nevertheless argued that contingent propositions can be known a priori. See discussions of this in Parkinson, *Logic and Reality,* p. 66, and Beck, *Early German Philosophy* (Cambridge, 1969), pp. 210-11.

13. *Philosophical Papers and Letters,* p. 286.

14. B. Russell, *Critical Examination of the Philosophy of Leibniz,* p. 20.

15. *New Essays Concerning Human Understanding,* IV, 1, §7.

16. Ibid., IV, 2, §1 (trans. Langley, pp. 404-5). See Margaret Wilson, "On Leibniz's Explication of 'Necessary Truth'," *Studia Leibnitiana Supplementa* 3 (1969): 50-63.

17. For Leibniz's criticisms of the Hobbesian theory which permitted nominal definitions to suffice, see *Philosophical Papers and Letters,* pp. 199, 355, 371. Against Locke on trifling propositions, see *New Essays,* II, 6, §27; III, 6, §§24 and 32; IV, 5, §§3-8, and Douglas Odegard, "Locke, Leibniz, and Identical Propositions," *Studia Leibnitiana* 1 (1969): 241-53.

18. Russell, *Critical Examination,* p. 18.

19. *Logical Papers,* trans. Parkinson (Oxford, 1966), pp. 64-65.

20. *Prolegomena,* §2.

21. See Gottfried Martin, *Kant: Ontologie und Wissenschaftstheorie* (4th ed., Berlin, 1969), p. 293; Winfried Lenders, *Die analytische Begriffs- und Urteilslehre von Leibniz u. Wolff* (Hildesheim: Olms, 1971), p. 158. On this point alone I disagree with Gram in his excellent introduction to the Lovejoy paper in *Kant: Disputed Questions,* p. 95.

22. *Vernünftige Gedanken von den Kräften des menschlichen Verstandes,* chapter 3, §§1, 2. It is this view which Kant criticizes in *K.d.r.V.* B §19.

23. *Logica,* §§262-64; *Psychologia Empirica,* §369.

24. See the quotation from Lovejoy in Gram, ed., *Kant: Disputed Questions,* 116n. and the immediately following passages in *Vernünftige Gedanken . . . ,* chapter 3, §§10 and 13; also, ibid., chapter 4, §21.

25. *Ontologia,* §48.

26. *Vernünftige Gedanken . . . ,* chapter 3, §10.

27. *K.d.r.V.* A274/B330.

28. Lovejoy, "Kant's Antithesis . . . ," p. 115.

29. Lambert to Kant, February 3, 1766; AA 10, 64; Zweig, *Kant's Philosophical Correspondence,* p. 51.

30. *Vernünftige Gedanken . . . ,* chapter 1, §§33.

31. *Logica,* §64.
32. *Ontologia,* §170.
33. Ibid., §§89 and 91.
34. Ibid., §92.
35. Lambert certainly did not see this criterion of possibility functioning in Wolff's own mathematics; see *Early German Philosophy,* p. 404.
36. *Vernünftige Gedanken . . .,* chapter 3, §13; *Logica,* §270.
37. *Logica,* §223.
38. Ibid., §273.
39. Ibid., §223.
40. Lovejoy, "Kant's Antithesis . . .," p. 117.
41. *Logica,* §§220-221.
42. *Vernünftige Gedanken . . .,* chapter 5, §6. Oddly enough, Kant regards the proposition "A triangle possesses three sides and three angles" as analytic (A716/B744). See G. Martin, *Kant: Ontologie . . .,* pp. 276-77.
43. *Vernünftige Gedanken . . .* chapter 4, §21, end.
44. *Ontologia* § 143; cf. § 546, note.
45. *Vernünftige Gedanken . . .* chapter 5, §§ 6, 7.
46. *K.d.r.V.* B2.
47. *Vernünftige Gedanken . . .,* chapter 5, §8. Other examples are: "Bodies have weight," and "Air is elastic"—examples Kant himself uses.
48. *Preliminary Discourse on Philosophy in General* (trans. R. J. Blackwell, [Indianapolis, 1963]), §6.
49. Crusius developed an idea which was present in the works of Clauberg, von Tschirnhaus, and Friedrich Adolf Hoffmann (see *Early German Philosophy,* pp. 185, 191-92, 302-3); later the same way of distinguishing two types of relations was followed by Johann Heinrich Lambert and Johann Heinrich Tetens (ibid., 406-7, 421, 425), but Kant had by then already learned the lesson from Crusius.
50. *Prolegomena,* trans. Beck, p. 8.
51. Letter of August 24, 1793 (AA 11, 444-45).
52. *Ontologia,* § 70.
53. *Weg zur Gewissheit,* §260.
54. *Entwurf der nothwendigen Vernunftwahrheiten,* §31.
55. Ibid., §15.
56. Kant to Reinhold, May 19, 1789 (AA 11, 41; Zweig, *Kant's Philosophical Correspondence,* p. 144); Reflexionen 4275 and 4446 (AA 17, 492-554); see also *Vorlesungen über Logik* (AA 9, 21).
57. *Versuch den Begriff der negativen Grössen in die Weltweisheit einzuführen,* 1763 (AA 2, 203).
58. Dieter Henrich, "Kants Denken 1762–63: Ueber den Ursprung der

Unterscheidung analytischer und synthetischer Urteile," in *Studien zu Kants philosophischer Entwicklung,* ed. Heimsoeth, Henrich, and Tonelli (Hildesheim, 1967), pp. 9-38; Gottfried Martin, *Kant: Ontologie* . . ., Teil III; Lewis White Beck, *Early German Philosophy,* pp. 441-46, 451-55.

59. Since this paper was written, Professor Henry E. Allison has published his translation of *Ueber eine Entdeckung* . . . with supplementary material and a historical and critical commentary: *The Kant-Eberhard Controversy* (Johns Hopkins University Press, 1973).

60. See Lewis White Beck's *Studies in the Philosophy of Kant,* pp. 81-84, 118-20 for comparison of Eberhard's strictures on Kant with those of C. I. Lewis. In that essay I deal largely with another problem raised by Maass, Eberhard, and Lewis, that of the variability and arbitrariness of the distinction between analytic and synthetic, which here I must pass over in silence.

61. Kant to Reinhold, May 12, 1789 (AA 11, 38; Zweig, *Kant's Philosophical Correspondence,* p. 141); Allison, *The Kant-Eberhard Controversy,* p. 164.

62. *Analysis of Knowledge and Valuation,* 89. S. G. E. Maass, "Ueber den höchsten Grundsatz der synthetischen-Urtheile," writing in Eberhard's *Philosophisches Magazin* (II [1790]: 186-231 at 197) and Eberhard's ally in the battle, distinguishes between immediate and mediate analytic judgments, corresponding exactly to Lewis's distinction. On Maass, see Allison, *The Kant-Eberhard Controversy,* pp. 42-45.

63. *Prolegomena,* §2, a.

64. *Ueber eine Entdeckung,* AA 8, 230, 242 (Allison, *The Kant-Eberhard Controversy,* pp. 142, 152); Eberhard, "Ueber die Unterscheidung der Urtheile in Analytische und Synthetische," *Philosophisches Magazin,* 1 (1780): 307-22, at 321.

65. *K.d.r.V.* A154/B193.

66. Eberhard, "Ueber die analytischen und synthetischen Urtheile zur Beantwortung des zweyten Abschnittes von H. Kants Streitschrift," *Philosophisches Magazin,* 3 (1791): 280-303 at 282, complains of this, saying that the presence or absence of intuition has nothing to do with the division of judgments. In "Weitere Ausführung der Untersuchung über die Unterscheidung der Urtheile in Analytische und Synthetische," ibid., 2 (1790): 285-315 at 299, Eberhard says that since he is convinced "dass die allgemeinen Principien der menschlichen Erkenntnis transcendentale Gültigkeit haben: so halte ich mich berechtigt, so lange mein Beweis von dieser transcendentalen Gültigkeit [sc., of the principle of sufficient reason derived from the law of contradiction] noch nicht widerlegt ist, einen jeden logischen Grund auch für einen Realgrund zu halten. . . ." It is the thesis of Lender's monograph *(Die analytische Begriffs- und Urteilslehre . . .)* that also in

Wolff the ground of distinction among the kinds of judgment is ontological, not epistemological or logical.

67. *K.d.r.V.* B40, A71/B96; *Vorlesungen über Logik,* §8; cf. Vaihinger, *Commentar zu Kants Kritik der reinen Vernunft* 1 (1881): 258.

68. Kant has often been criticized for holding two criteria of analyticity, the phenomenological or introspective ("actually thought" in the concept of the subject) and the logical (testable by the law that the contradiction of an analytical judgment is self-contradictory). Here we have a clear indication that when these criteria give conflicting answers, Kant accepts the latter as prevailing. On the other hand, it is equally clear from their dispute that, when they conflict, Eberhard must use the former in justifying his considering a judgment *per attributum* to be synthetic.

69. *Ueber eine Entdeckung,* AA 8, 230 (Allison, *The Kant-Eberhard Controversy,* p. 143). The distinction is (naturally) denied by Eberhard in his reply, "Ueber die analytischen und synthetischen Urtheile, zur Beantwortung des zweyten Abschnittes von H. Prof. Kants Streitschrift," *Philosophisches Magazin* 3 (1791): 280-303, in particular p. 302.

70. *K.d.r.V.* A598/B626. "Praedicatum logicum kan [sic!] analytisch sein; determinatio est praedicatumo syntheticum." Reflexion 5701 (AA 18, 330).

71. *Ueber eine Entdeckung,* AA 8, 242 (Allison, *The Kant-Eberhard Controversy,* p. 152); letter to Reinhold, May 12, 1789 (Zweig, *Kant's Philosophical Correspondence,* p. 140; Allison, *The Kant-Eberhard Controversy,* pp. 163-64).

72. *K.d.r.V.* A292/B348.

73. Ibid., A218/B265.

74. Kant may perhaps have confused Eberhard by calling real essence "die innere Möglichkeit des Begriffes" or "interna possibilitas" and distinguishing it from the "logisches Wesen" (*Ueber eine Entdeckung,* AA 8, 229). By "innere Möglichkeit des Begriffes" he actually means "innere Möglichkeit *des Objektes* des Begriffes." This is made clear in the manuscripts Kant prepared to help Schulz in Schulz's reply to Eberhard (AA 20, 376, first full paragraph); similar usage in *Vorlesungen über Logik* (AA 9, 61); *Vorlesungen über Metaphysik* (ed. Pölitz, 1821), p. 38; *K.d.r.V.,* A676/B703; A816/B844. *Einzig möglicher Beweisgrund* (AA 2, 77-78, 162) distinguishes "innere Möglichkeit" from "das Logische in der Möglichkeit" and identifies the former with the "Wesen der Dinge." I have examined all these passages in "Lovejoy as a Critic of Kant," *Journal of the History of Ideas* 33 (1972): 471-84, in particular pp. 482-83.

75. *K.d.r.V.* A728/B756.

THE MYTH OF DOUBLE AFFECTION

Moltke S. Gram

The theory of double affection (call it *DA* for short) is a classical attempt to rescue Kant's account of perceptual awareness from what is alleged to be a glaring inconsistency. But *DA* is a remedy worse than the disease it is supposed to cure. The problem confronting *DA* arises with the notion of affection and can be stated in the form of a dilemma neither horn of which is compatible with Kant's theory of perception. The problem generates the dilemma in the following way. To be affected by anything, so the Kantian account goes, is to experience what Kant calls "[t]he effect of an object upon the faculty of representation."[1] The notion of affection does not, however, become fully clear unless we can specify the kind of object which can stand in such a relation to our sensibility. There are two possibilities open to the theory neither of which would seem to make the notion of affection any more intelligible than the other. That is, I shall argue, the dilemma to which *DA* has been proposed as an answer. But I shall also argue that the dilemma is ultimately spurious.

Let me begin the construction of the dilemma by ignoring a complication in the notion of affection which is irrelevant to the issue facing *DA*. Kant describes affection as the experience of the *effect* of an object on our sensory apparatus. The dilemma facing Kant's theory has nothing to do with the quite separate issue of whether what is related to sensibility is the effect of an object rather than the object itself. The issue concerns the nature of the object which is immediately present to perceptual awareness rather than the causal relation in which it might stand to some further object.

With this restriction in mind consider what the dilemma is. Suppose we say that what affects our sensibility is a thing in itself.[2] This account of what affects us, however, prevents us from distinguishing between a case in which somebody perceives an object and the quite different case in which an object exerts a merely causal influence on the body of the perceiver. This can be seen by consulting an elementary fact of perception. The fact is that to perceive anything is to perceive it under a certain description. If this were not the case, then we could not distinguish between the perceiving of one object rather than another. But if we must always perceive something under a description, to say that we are affected by a thing in itself when we perceive anything would imply that we perceive that objects satisfy certain descriptions. And this would contradict the claim that we cannot be perceptually acquainted with a thing in itself.

It will do no good here to say that a thing in itself can act upon our sensory organs even though we cannot perceive it to satisfy any description at all. If this were the case, we would not be able to distinguish between a situation in which an object causally affects our bodies in certain ways and we do not perceive the effects of that action from the quite different situation in which the object exerts such an influence and we do perceive it. This, then, is the first horn of the dilemma. If the affection relation is to hold between a thing in itself and an act of perceptual awareness, we would have to be able to perceive things in themselves under descriptions appropriate to them or obliterate the distinction between causation and perceptual awareness. In either case, the candidature of things in themselves for one of the relata of the affection relation would only serve to destroy the theory on which it is erected.

There is, however, another candidate for one of the relata of the affection relation. Suppose we say that what affects our sensibility is a phenomenal object, allowing anything which has spatial or temporal characteristics to count as such an object.[3] This alternative, it would seem, succeeds in rescuing the theory of affection from the disastrous implication that we can perceive objects which cannot be in our sensory fields.

The gain, however, is illusory. Such a claim would conflict with Kant's assertion that space and time are forms of our sensibility. Consider how the conflict arises. Sensibility, we are told, is "[t]he capacity (receptivity) for receiving representations through the mode in which we are affected by objects."[4] But what Kant calls the mode of affection here is the form of sensuous intuition, which is, in turn, the way in which the subject is affected.[5] And this merely implies that affection is to be partially defined in terms of a relation in which an object stands to certain spatio-temporal forms; hence, there can be no such relation between a *phenomenal* object and such forms. For the relation is specified in terms of a connection between an object and these forms, not in terms of an object exhibiting these forms and sensibility. What makes a phenomenal object an even unlikelier candidate for one of the relata of the affection relation is that such an assumption leads us back to the equally unacceptable candidature of the thing in itself. If the object which affects the forms of our sensibility cannot itself have spatio-temporal characteristics, then what affects us must, on Kant's theory, be a thing in itself. Thus replacing things in themselves with phenomenal objects merely returns us to all of the difficulties of the first horn of the dilemma.

The theory of *DA* purports to supply a remedy for the foregoing dilemma. It purports to show that both things in themselves and phenomenal objects can affect the perceiving subject, albeit in different ways. The claim for double affection is made to rest on two kinds of evidence. There is, first, the claim that assuming *DA* defuses the dilemma which I have just sketched. And, secondly, there is the claim that several of the most characteristic doctrines of the *Kritik* imply the existence of double affection.[6] But neither of these claims is true. For one thing, the *Kritik* does not commit Kant to such a doctrine. For another, imputing it to Kant's theory of perception does not remove the dilemma facing the theory. This does not, however, leave us with an insuperable dilemma. For what generates the dilemma is a confusion between two different conceptions of what a thing in itself is and how it relates to our sensibility. The confusion is not Kant's. It is, rather, the result of an imperfect understanding of the concept of intuition in his theory of perception.

1. The Principal Parts of *DA*

Let me begin by formulating the claims which proponents of *DA* have traditionally tried to defend. I distinguish three such claims:

1. Appearances in themselves stand in a relation of empirical affection to the empirical ego.[7]
2. Things in themselves transcendently affect the ego in itself.[8]
3. The result of (2) is the world of perceptual objects which are presented to the empirical ego.[9]

Consider how these claims contrive to remove the dilemma. We are faced with the problem that neither phenomenal objects nor things in themselves can affect our sensibility. The former cannot do this because they cannot be perceived; the latter because it leads us back to things in themselves. *DA* must, accordingly, show how something can affect our sensibility without acquiring spatio-temporal characteristics. It must also show how what we do perceive to have such characteristics can affect our sensibility without once again driving us back to the untenable position that what we are perceiving in such a case is something that lacks such characteristics. In order to accomplish this, the demonstration relies on the crucial distinction between empirical and transcendent affection. The former does not require that the objects in our sensory field lack spatio-temporal characteristics. And the latter countenances the existence of objects which affect ego in themselves; it thereby seeks to avoid the difficulty issuing from the claim that things in themselves affect our sensibility. The claim has initial plausibility. If affection can hold between things in themselves and egos that are not in time and space, the dilemma I have just sketched would seem to be removed. For we would seem not to face the problem of an object which must be but cannot be spatio-temporal if we are to meet the requirements of perceiving an object. Things in themselves affect the ego in itself; phenomenal things, the phenomenal ego. One and the same object would no longer be pressed into the impossible service of being perceived to have spatiotemporal characteristics and being perceived not to have them. But the distinction between two kinds of affection is a myth. It is not implied by the other parts of Kant's theory of perception. Nor can it escape the dilemma facing that theory. Consider the evidence for such a distinction.

2. The Status of Appearances in Themselves

DA relies essentially on the distinction between what Adickes calls an appearance in itself and a thing in itself. The term "appearance in itself" is, however, an invention of the *DA* theory. It is not to be found in so many words in the *Kritik*. But there is another term which is both present in so many words in the *Kritik* and which designates a state of affairs which the *DA* theorist exploits as *prima facie* evidence for his theory. In the *Kritik* Kant speaks of an appearance as a thing in itself in the empirical understanding *(ein Ding an sich selbst im empirischen Verstande)*.[10] This is the textual foundation for claiming, as the *DA* theorist does, that there are appearances in themselves. For there are things, if the theory is right, which both have the properties of space and time—existing, as Kant says, *im empirischen Verstande*—and which are nonetheless things in themselves.

The notion of an appearance in itself, founded though it is in the text, still functions as a theoretical term for *DA*. It is a way of characterizing a situation acknowledged by Kant's description of the perceptual situation which generates a critical difficulty for that theory. That there are appearances in themselves is crucial to *DA* if it is to make a serious claim to our attention. For the plausibility of that theory derives from the fact that there are entities which both have spatio-temporal characteristics and are relata of the affection relation. The critical issue can be put in this way: *DA* seems to be required once you say that something with spatio-temporal characteristics stands in the affection relation to a perceiver and, further, that what stands in such a relation to a perceiver is really a thing in itself. These claims generate a contradiction, for something cannot stand in the affection relation to a perceiver and be both a thing in itself and a phenomenal entity. That is the difficulty which the notion of an appearance in itself signals.

DA depends, then, on the notion of an appearance in itself even though that notion surfaces in the *Kritik* in different semantical garb. The absence of the phrase "appearance in itself" does not prevent the issue to which *DA* is meant as an answer from arising. But there is, nonetheless, an argument to show that the very notion of an appearance in itself is internally coherent and, further, that no theory—not even one as complicated as *DA*—is needed to solve a problem in Kant's theory of perception. The argument runs like this: The very notion of an appearance in itself is said to be self-contradictory. To say that anything is an appearance is, according to this argument, to say that somebody stands in an epistemic relation to whatever is called an appearance. Whatever we choose to call an appearance cannot, therefore, be anything in itself just because it cannot be what it is outside of the relation in which it stands to a perceiver. But to say of anything that it has some status implies that it can satisfy the description it does outside of the relation in which it may stand to any perceiver. An appearance cannot satisfy this condition; therefore, there can be no appearances in themselves. And if there can be no such entitites, there is no textual necessity to import a theory like *DA* to account for the existence of such entities to our sensibility.

The notion of an appearance in itself cannot be undermined so easily. The attempt to avert the difficulties of *DA* by disqualifying the very notion of an appearance in itself breaks down on a fatal ambiguity inherent in that notion. Something can stand in an epistemic relation to a perceiver and be called an appearance. But whatever might stand in that relation to a perceiver is not an appearance but something which can be neutrally described as an object. In this case what we perceive can stand outside the epistemic relation it may have to a perceiver without ceasing to be what it is. This is not the case, however, in the situation which I have just described as a case of an *appearance* which appears to somebody.

The distinction I have just made shows the true threat of the problem of which *DA* is one solution. It shows that something can appear to us without being an appearance. The notion of an appearance in itself entails a contradiction only on the assumption that an appearance is an object which stands in some relation to a perceiver. But if that object is not an appearance but, rather, something else which is not essentially described as an appearance, then what stands in such a relation is not an appearance but something else which can exist and satisfy a description outside that relation. What appears, in other words, is not an appearance. It is an object that appears. And this is what frees the notion of an appearance in itself from the difficulties that would otherwise undermine it at the very outset.

The notion of an appearance in itself does not render the *DA* theory superfluous. The notion is used to support *DA* by the following line of argument.[11] If there were only one kind of affection, there would be only one kind of object affecting the ego. But, so the argument goes, Kant provides two kinds of objects which affect the self. There are, in the first place, things in themselves which affect the self. There are, in the second place, appearances in themselves which act on our sensibility. Appearances in themselves exist independently of the sensory apparatus of whoever perceives them. They are, therefore, independent of whatever characteristics attach to our sensory receptors. But at the same time appearances in themselves also have spatio-temporal properties. The former characteristic enables them to affect our sensibility; the latter, to be directly present in our sensory field without contradicting the claim that things in themselves cannot be objects of such awareness. Appearances in themselves are like things in themselves in that they are independent of the existence of our sensory receptors. They are unlike things in themselves in that they have spatio-temporal characteristics.

There are two kinds of evidence on which *DA* draws to support this use of appearances in themselves in Kant's theory of perception. In the first place, we are reminded that Kant cites the example of a rose which can appear to different observers in different ways depending upon the peculiarities of our sensory apparatus.[12] The rose is an appearance because it has spatio-temporal characteristics; but since it can appear to various observers in different ways under different circumstances, it can affect the sensibility of different observers in various ways without ceasing to be a spatio-temporal object.

The same point can be put in a different way. Objects that can appear to have characteristics that they lack show that they are independent of the features of our sensibility. That fact, as far as the present example goes, is enough to show that there can be appearances that share at least one feature in common with things in themselves; namely, both exist independently of the characteristics of our sensibility. But at the same time appearances in themselves still retain spatio-temporal properties.

Does this kind of example provide evidence for *DA*? I think not. At A28/B45 Kant begins to discuss the variability of our perceptions of color and concludes that they

> cannot rightly be regarded as properties of things, but only as changes in the subject, changes which may, indeed, be different for different men. In such examples as these, that which is originally itself only appearance, for instance, a rose, is being treated by the empirical understanding as a thing in itself, which, nevertheless, can appear differently to every observer. The transcendental concept of appearances in space, on the other hand, is a reminder that nothing in space is a thing in itself, that space is not a form inhering in things in themselves as their intrinsic property.

What this shows is that physical objects like roses can exist independently of the accidental features of the sensory apparatus of each observer. An object can appear to have properties it lacks, for example, if the organism of the observer is diseased or temporarily altered by some other means. It does not show that spatio-temporal objects affect the self in one way and things in themselves in another. The same fact of perceptual relativity could be explained on the assumption that what appears to our sensibility is a thing in itself; hence, the distinction that Kant draws between what is a thing in itself for the empirical understanding and what counts as a thing in itself *simpliciter* can draw no support from the fact of perceptual variability.

The same point can be put in a different way. The rose example shows that phenomenal objects can appear to have properties which they lack. A rose that is red can, under certain circumstances of perception, appear to be, say, yellow. But this neither requires nor supports the distinction between two kinds of affection. All it requires is that we recognize the distinction between affecting and appearing. To affect our perceptual apparatus is for an object to stand in a relation to our sensibility which, in our case, is characterized by space and time. Yet the object given to us under these forms can appear to be other than it is and might still be a thing in itself. To say that something is a thing in itself for the empirical understanding does not, therefore, imply two relations of affection. All it does imply is that spatio-temporal objects independent of our sensory apparatus can appear to have properties they lack. And this is silent about what it is, exactly, that can appear other than it is.

This is not all. Even if you say that appearances in themselves affect us in one way and things in themselves in another, the dilemma with which we began still faces Kant's theory once you have imported such a distinction into his argument. Suppose we say that a thing in itself transcendently affects the ego in itself and an appearance in itself empirically affects the empirical ego. The dilemma breaks out all over again with respect to the notion of an appearance in itself. If an appearance in itself is just a thing in itself affecting the ego, we have the difficulty of explaining how things in themselves are knowable. And if an appearance in itself is a spatio-temporal object affecting the forms of our sensibility, then we have the equally great difficulty of explaining how we can avoid the assumption of a thing in itself which stands in the affection relation to the perceiver.

But *DA* dies hard. Suppose we try to repair the foregoing difficulty by invoking the distinction between two kinds of ego. What faces *DA* is the difficulty of explaining how an appearance in itself can affect our sensibility without resolving itself into a relation of a thing in itself to the perceiver. It might be argued, however, that an appearance in itself affects the empirical ego while a thing in itself affects the ego in itself. The claim, crucial to *DA*, that there are two kinds of affection would then be made to rest on the difference between two kinds of ego. A thing in itself would not, accordingly, affect our sensibility. For it would stand in relation only to the ego in itself. What does affect our sensibility is an appearance in itself; and this, so the argument might run, no longer requires a *DA* theorist to admit that all cases of affection are ultimately relations of things in themselves to the forms of our sensibility. And so, the conclusion would seem to be that *DA* can remove the dilemma facing Kant's theory of perception.

Invoking the distinction between two kinds of ego serves, however, only to delay the demise of *DA*. The problem that arises for the *objects* of perceptual awareness is merely transferred to the *subjects* of that awareness. Consider how this comes about. What distinguishes the ego in itself from the empirical ego is that it can apprehend individuals without the forms of space and time which characterize our sensibility. But both still have something in common: Both must have some forms of sensibility or other. Kant does not explicitly claim this; but an argument can be constructed to show that his distinction between positive and negative noumena commits him to it. A negative noumenon is anything just insofar as it is not the object of our sensuous intuition; a positive noumenon, an object of a non-sensuous intuition.[13]

Let us suppose, as *DA* requires us to do, that transcendent affection is some kind of epistemic relation holding between a thing in itself and the ego in itself. What should be noticed here is that, even in the case of transcendent affection, there is a kind of intuition. And this requires that there be a sensibility for the ego in itself with characteristics of its own. If this were not the case, then *DA* could not explain, as it must, how transcendent affection gives the ego a relation to a *particular* rather than, say, only to a concept. The doctrine of transcendent affection requires the notion of a positive noumenon. Without such a notion the theory must also recognize, not the mere absence of sensibility, but merely a different kind of sensibility characterized by its own forms.[14]

The distinction between transcendent and empirical affection must be drawn, then, in terms of two ways in which particulars are received. The distinction cannot be drawn in terms of the presence or absence of any intuitive faculty at all. But once it is seen that even an ego in itself has a sensibility, the problem which the distinction between two kinds of ego was introduced to solve breaks out all over again with respect to an ego which does not have our forms of intuition. Even if we assume that the ego itself lacks the forms of sensibility which distinguish it from the empirical ego, we must assume that it has some forms of sensibility or other. The rejection of this assumption would prevent the ego in itself from being affected at all. But the acceptance of this assumption would merely raise all of the problems facing the notion of an appearance in itself at another level. What makes the notion so problematic is that, as I have argued, we are forced to account for it in terms of the relation in which something not having the forms of our sensibility stands to those forms.

Consider how this recapitulation comes about. The dilemma to which *DA* is supposed to be the solution arises over the relation of sensibility to the doctrine of affection. On the one hand, the object affecting us would seem to be a thing in itself—which is impossible because we would then have to perceive something which, on Kant's theory, we cannot. On the other hand, what stands in that relation to us would seem necessarily to be what Kant calls a phenomenal object—which is impossible because affection is defined as the relation of an object to the forms of our sensibility; hence, that relation precludes the object's having spatial or temporal characteristics. What generates the foregoing dilemma is Kant's assessment of the forms of sensibility. The difficulty in finding an acceptable relatum to stand in the affection relation to an ego issues from the fact that any candidate would seem both to have and not to have the characteristics of sensibility. And this problem does not disappear by appealing to the notion of transcendent affection even though the forms of such a sensibility would be different from those of the empirical ego.[15] They are, after all, still forms which qualify the way in which the ego in itself must be affected by a thing in itself. Thus a change in the character of sensibility does not give *DA* a way of removing the dilemma. Both kinds of ego must have forms of sensibility if they are to be affected by *particulars*.

All that an appeal to two kinds of ego can accomplish for the *DA* theorist, then, is to show that both kinds of affection must inevitably apply to each kind of ego—which is merely to perpetuate the problem that the distinction must eliminate. I conclude, therefore, that Kant's distinction between what are things in themselves for the empirical understanding and what are transcendent things in themselves fails to imply a corresponding distinction between two kinds of affection.

To distinguish between an appearance in itself and the variable circumstances of perceiving it lends no more support to the *DA* theorist. For the character of the appearing relation and its relata are precisely what is at stake here. Nor, finally, does the dilemma confronting the notion of an appearance in itself in Kant's theory of perception disappear if we allow ourselves to impute two kinds of affection to Kant's theory. Such a step merely raises the same problem all over again with respect to the relation between a thing in itself and an ego in itself.

There is, however, a second kind of example which Kant gives as a case of an appearance in itself. He cites a rainbow as a case of an appearance in itself, contrasting the way in which it appears to us with the rain constituting the object which appears. Thus he says that the "rainbow in a sunny shower may be called mere appearance, and the rain the thing itself."[16] This must be sharply distinguished from the rose example. For they give us very different grounds for believing in appearances in themselves. In the former case, perceptual *properties* of a particular vary with changing perceptual conditions. In the latter, the distinction holds between the micro- and macro-structures of one and the same *particular*. But, as the *DA* theorist quickly points out, even the micro-structure of rainbows has spatio-temporal properties. There is, so it is concluded, a relation of empirical affection between the micro-structures of phenomenal objects and the forms of our sensibility. The micro-structure of objects like rainbows exists independently of our forms of intuition. It is, in other words, an object which can exist independently of our sensory apparatus while at the same time having spatio-temporal characteristics.

The distinction between micro- and macro-constituents of an object is, however, useless to the *DA* theorist: It confuses causation with affection.[17] The rain is the partial cause of the rainbow we might see in our visual field. What stands in a relation to the forms of our sensibility is the rainbow and not the rain. For the rain does not generate the rainbow by acting on our sensory mechanism. It produces something else that does. It is about the rainbow, not the rain, that we must ask what its relation to that sensory mechanism is. And it is no answer to this objection to say that the cause of the effect which does act on our sensory mechanism is itself an item having spatio-temporal location. All this shows is that the various items of our spatio-temporal world can be related one to another as cause to effect. It does not show that the notion of an appearance in itself demands a theory of double affection but merely that one phenomenal item can cause another phenomenal item to occur.

But this is not the only reason for rejecting the claim, crucial to a *DA* theory, that the distinction between such entities as rain and rainbows requires the further distinction between two kinds of affection. There are two alternatives in characterizing the rainbow case which are conjointly exhaustive and neither of which establishes the existence of double affection. We may suppose either that the rainbow we see in our visual field is the same as the rain or that it is numerically different from the rain. Neither option implies *DA*. Take them in turn. Suppose we say that the rainbow and the rain are literally one and the same item. This would only obliterate the distinction between an appearance in itself and how it appears to us. For the rain as over against the rainbow would be the object that would occupy our perceptual fields. But in that case what was supposed to be an appearance in itself would really be an appearance *simpliciter*—which would not support the claim that appearances are items which can appear to us other than they are. And it would also cancel out the necessity to import the distinction between empirical and transcendent affection into Kant's theory of perception in order to explain the relation between that percipient and what he immediately perceives on the other.

All that remains to *DA* is to assume that the two items are numerically diverse. Yet, even this shows, at most, that one spatio-temporal item can cause another. The very fact that both items have spatio-temporal qualities shows that an account of the relation between the two requires something more than the forms of our sensibility. For both items satisfy spatio-temporal descriptions. To show, in other words, that one item in nature *causes* another is not to show that the two items *affect* us in different ways. Causation is not affection, empirical or otherwise. And this, in turn, shows that no double affection takes place in either case.[18]

I conclude, then, that Kant's distinctions between appearances and appearances in themselves, appearances and appearances of appearances, and appearances and things in themselves for the empirical understanding neither imply DA nor require the distinction between two kinds of affection in order to be made intelligible. They do not, as I have been arguing, imply DA. For the part of Kant's theory of perception to which a DA theorist appeals really consists of nothing more than the recognition of the phenomenon of perceptual variability. Whatever the problems which this fact raises, they cannot be removed by imputing DA to Kant. For such an imputation, as I have also been arguing, merely reproduces the problem it was meant to solve. Nor, finally, does the distinction between micro- and macro-structures of perceptual objects require the adoption of DA. For in this case what is baptized as a distinction between two kinds of affection is really only a distinction between causation and affection.

3. Ideality and Subjectivity

The notion of an appearance in itself present in Kant's theory of perception is not, however, the only evidence to which DA theorists have appealed. Kant calls some of the items of our experience ideal and contrasts these with what he calls merely subjective items.[19] DA theorists like Erich Adickes claim that this distinction collapses without the recognition of two kinds of affection. And from this they infer that the ideal-subjective distinction implies DA.[20] The argument for this conclusion runs as follows. Kant says that items like space and time are transcendentally ideal.[21] But he also says that secondary properties like colors, tastes, and smells are merely subjective. And this is what generates the problem. Both ideality and subjectivity betoken the fact that whatever has either is dependent in some way on the characteristics of our sensory apparatus. There remains, however, the crucial distinction between the sense in which each kind of item is dependent. If something is transcendentally ideal, it depends for its existence upon a generic character of our sensibility as such. But whatever is merely subjective is dependent upon the peculiarities of some perceiver.

But, so the argument concludes, if this distinction is to be preserved, we must attribute *DA* to Kant.

Does such a distinction require *DA*? I think not. Consider how Kant introduces the distinction between subjectivity and ideality. This can be inferred from what he says at A28/B44. In the first place, anything is ideal whenever it is the basis for verification of a synthetic a priori judgment. This is not the case with an item of experience which is merely subjective. In the second place, something is ideal whenever it is a necessary condition for any object's being presented to us in intuition. Distinguish, for example, between the status which Kant gives to space and, say, a color. Both are dependent for their existence, according to Kant, on our sensory apparatus. But space fulfills both of the foregoing conditions, while color can be absent from the content of our experience without making it impossible for us to experience any object whatever.

But, as it stands, the distinction between subjectivity and ideality alone offers no support to the *DA* theorist. That something in our experience is neither the necessary condition for our experiencing any object at all nor the basis for the verification of a synthetic a priori judgment does not require a distinction between two ways of our being affected by objects. It requires, at most, the recognition of two different roles which the items affecting our sensibility play in our experience. And this is still compatible with our being affected in only one way.

The distinction between subjectivity and ideality is, however, also linked with the distinction between primary and secondary properties.[22] What Kant calls secondary properties are subjective in that they allegedly have an origin different from ideal items.[23] The secondary properties of an object are the partial result of the characteristics of our sensibility. But they are also partially the result of the action of the primary properties of an object on our sensibility.[24] And yet both primary and secondary properties belong only to bodies which are spatio-temporally located. To separate primary from secondary properties as Kant does, so the *DA* theorist's argument runs, assumes that there are qualities of spatio-temporal objects which act upon the perceiver to produce his experience of secondary qualities.

Thus while both kinds of quality are ideal in that they are instantiated by objects which also have spatio-temporal characteristics, secondary qualities are subjective in that they are the effects of the causal action of primary properties on the sensibility of the perceiver. Primary qualities empirically affect the perceiver because they are in space and time. But the objects having such qualities transcendently affect the ego because they lack spatio-temporal characteristics.[25]

The fact is, however, that Kant's distinction between subjectivity and ideality does not require *DA*. Consider the distinction between primary and secondary qualities. Let us suppose that there are bodies having, say, such properties as size, shape, and solidity which, in turn, cause us to experience objects as having color, taste, smell, and sound. This distinction does not require *DA*. At most it requires that we recognize the existence of certain powers or dispositional properties which cause us to experience other properties. And this requires us, again, to distinguish between causation and affection. Primary properties may *cause* us to experience secondary properties; but this does not imply that they *affect* our forms of sensibility. They may cause sensations of certain kinds to occur in us. But this is not so much evidence of the existence of a relation called empirical affection as it is of the fact of causation in our perception.

That primary and secondary qualities are distinguishable does not, however, prove even that our perception of secondary qualities is *caused* by the primary properties of the bodies we perceive. That something is a primary quality of a body does not prevent it from being the content of an act of perceptual awareness. We can perceive the primary qualities of a body simultaneously with the secondary qualities which that body has. That both kinds of property can be simultaneously present in our sensory field shows that they affect us in the same way. Thus even though it may be the case that a body's possession of both kinds of property is to be explained in terms of properties it has which cannot be presented in a spatio-temporal framework, the distinction between primary and secondary properties does not of itself demand a distinction between two kinds of affection.

4. Individuals and Spatiality

The distinction between secondary and primary qualities does not, I have argued, demand a distinction between empirical and transcendent affection. This still does not exhaust the evidence on which the *DA* theorist relies. Two kinds of affection are required, we are told, if we are to account for the diversity of spatial shapes which the objects of our apprehension have.[26] To say, as Kant does, that space is a form of our sensibility is merely to say that it characterizes our apprehension of things in outer sense. But it does not explain why the figures of things we perceive in space have a variety of shapes. Kant explains this in two divergent ways. On the one hand, he claims that appearances in themselves determine the difference between the spatial characteristics of perceptual objects.[27] On the other hand, however, he says that what accounts for the very same fact is the character of things in themselves.[28] But he cannot say both. If what is called an appearance in itself is supposed to account for such features of our experience as spatial diversity, then there is no need to import things in themselves to account for an account that has already been given. And if things in themselves are supposed to account for the fact of spatial diversity, then there is no need to import appearances in themselves to accomplish the same task.

The *DA* theorist offers the following solution. What determines the diversity of characteristics exhibited by spatial objects is, according to *DA*, the way things in themselves are constituted.[29] But this does not contradict the claim that appearances in themselves determine such characteristics. Things in themselves *remotely* determine the spatial characteristics of the things we intuit. What we intuit in that intuition, however, is *proximately* determined by an appearance in itself. Kant does not, according to *DA*, say that both things in themselves and appearances in themselves account for spatial differences in things. That one spatial configuration is different from another is supposedly explained by the fact that some properties of a thing in itself are different from the properties which other things in themselves have. The difference in spatial properties exhibited by appearances in themselves is explained by the existence of a corresponding difference in the order of things in themselves. The contradiction disappears, according to DA, once we recognize that things in themselves transcendently affect the ego in itself and appearances in themselves empirically affect the empirical ego. Since they stand in relation to different things, the contradiction between claiming that appearances in themselves and things in themselves account for the diversity of spatial figures disappears.

The appeal to Kant's variant explanations of the diversity of shape breaks down on two crucial difficulties. It is not implied by Kant's explanations. And, what is even more damaging to DA, imputing that theory to Kant does not succeed in removing the alleged contradiction. Take these in turn. You can hold without contradiction that both things in themselves and appearances in themselves account for the diversity of spatial figures. Nothing in the concept of an appearance in itself forbids analyzing it as the content of an intuition generated whenever a thing in itself affects our sensibility.[30] There are, as I have already pointed out, philosophical difficulties with this account. But a contradiction in Kant's account of the diversity of spatial figures is not among them. What remains is to explicate the relation between an appearance in itself and a thing in itself. But the difficulty that attends such an explication must not be confused with the quite separate difficulty issuing from the claim that Kant's account of spatial diversity entails a contradiction. The former arises for Kant's account of affection in general. But the latter can at best provide fresh evidence for the problem. And since no such contradiction exists, there is no fresh evidence to support the claim that Kant's theory implies DA; hence, the Kantian explanation of spatial diversity does *not* imply DA.

But let us suppose, for the sake of the argument, that there is a genuine conflict with Kant's account of spatial diversity. Does DA remove that conflict? I think not. First we must locate the place where the conflict arises. I have already shown how to interpret the relation between a thing in itself and an appearance in itself which does not entail such a conflict. Yet one might argue that, so long as we impute to Kant only one kind of affection, both a thing in itself and an appearance in itself could not stand in that relation to somebody perceiving spatial shapes.

An appearance in itself is in space and time. They are the conditions of our ability to be affected at all. But this is not the case with a thing in itself. To work with only one notion of affection would, accordingly, conflict with the claim that a thing in itself and an appearance in itself can both affect us.

What does *DA* offer to relieve this conflict? We are given, naturally, two relations of affection: one, relating the thing in itself to the ego in itself; the other, relating the appearance in itself to the empirical ego. This may remove the contradiction at one level. But what results only reproduces the problem it was supposed to solve. The existence of a sensibility even for the ego in itself as a necessary condition of nonsensuously intuiting anything only permits us to raise the difference between two kinds of account of the diversity of what we see all over again for that ego. For such an appeal merely resurrects the distinction between the way in which something is constituted apart from any sensibility whatever and the way in which that object appears to a perceiver. This, I have argued, follows from the fact that a noumenal ego must have a sensibility in order to be affected by a thing in itself. Since all of the distinctions which are made with respect to our sensibility and the objects which are given to it can be made with a noumenal sensibility, an appeal to a difference of affection cannot remove the alleged contradiction in Kant's account of spatial diversity. *DA* cannot, therefore, be confirmed in virtue of its power to remove that alleged conflict in Kant's account.

5. The Affinity of Appearances

But the diversity of spatial characteristics attaching to the objects we perceive is not the only difficulty which the *DA* theorist claims to remove from Kant's theory of perception. There is, it is claimed, a conflict internal to Kant's doctrine of affinity.[31] Kant says, on the one hand, that all of our knowledge of natural laws must be derived from our experience of events in nature.[32] This follows from what Kant says about the nature of the affinity of appearances: There must be an objective ground on the basis of which we synthesize the perceptual manifold in the way we do.[33] What distinguishes a mere succession of perceptions from an ordered sequence of perceptions is that there is a ground in the object for the latter while there is none in the former. Kant claims, on this view, that our ability to distinguish between a synthesis governed by law and one that cannot be subjected to any rule is founded on something which is present in the object.

This is not all that Kant says. He also claims that all laws or rules governing the synthesis of perceptual manifolds are introduced into our perception of nature by the self.[34] That we order a manifold in one way rather than in another is explained, on this view, by a capacity of the self and not by whatever properties there are in the object. The *DA* theorist offers to reconcile this conflict in the following way.[35] What *DA* calls the objective affinity underlying sequences of all our perceptions is to be explained by the action of the ego in itself on appearances in themselves.[36] This supposedly explains the independent ground for the rules of synthesis we apply to objects. But all synthesis is, nonetheless, subjective in that what we call an appearance in itself is really a construction which we make out of a series of perceptions.[37] In this way, then, *DA* seeks to resolve the conflict in Kant's theory of affinity.

But here, again, *DA* fails. And, again, it fails on two counts. For one thing, *DA* is powerless to remove the apparent conflict between the claims Kant makes about the sources of the rules of synthesis. For another, what the *DA* theorist calls a conflict between two grounds of rules of synthesis is illusory. Let us assume, in the first place, that the ego in itself somehow acts in such a way as to bring about the affinity of appearances which justifies the application of one rule of synthesis rather than another. This would only raise the original problem all over again. What generates the problem? According to the *DA* theorist, it is the difficulty of reconciling the existence of an affinity of appearances with the fact that all rules for combining the manifold are supplied by the ego. But to say that the ego in itself generates the order in the sequences which appearances in themselves present to us merely allows us to raise our original question all over again at the level of the activity of the ego in itself; the question, namely, of how to distinguish between the basis for an objective ordering of appearances and an ordering that is imposed on the sequence of appearances by the ego. To invoke an action of the ego in itself on appearances in themselves to explain this distinction merely requires an explanation at another level of the distinction between those rules which the ego in itself imposes on appearances in themselves and those it does not.

Yet the fact remains that there is no contradiction requiring the remedy offered by *DA*. No contradiction arises if you say, as Kant admittedly does, both that the self generates the rules according to which it synthesizes a perceptual manifold and that the self must always rely upon the way the world is in order to know what these rules are. This apparent contradiction dissolves once we distinguish between two different but mutually compatible claims. To say that all synthesis is an activity of the ego and not given to us by the objects we synthesize is to put forward a thinly disguised tautology: What is claimed is something about the essential feature of how we must come to know anything which is given to us in perception. To say that all synthesis is the work of the intellect is merely to claim that the way which we have of perceiving things is to unite a series of presentations. And this serves only to tell us that the self must rely on some activity of synthesis or other in order to perceive anything. It does not follow, however, that the rules in virtue of which that capacity is exercised on any particular occasion are also generated by the self. And to say that the rules of synthesis of the various objects we are given are derived from an affinity of appearances merely formulates the claim that the distinction between correctly and incorrectly synthesizing any given manifold cannot be derived from a general analysis of the nature of synthesis as such.

What emerges from the foregoing distinction is this: Our perceptual apparatus consists of whatever we bring with us to the apprehension of the objects which are given to us. This consists of the generic characteristics of the capacity to synthesize any manifold at all. These are rules for combining any manifold at all. But there are also rules for correctly combining any *given* manifold. There are, I conclude, general rules that any act of synthesis must satisfy in order to count as an act of synthesis. There are also specific rules which an act of synthesis must satisfy if it is to govern a correct apprehension of a given *kind* of object. The former are put into nature in that they prescribe how we must go about the apprehension of any perceptual object. The latter are derived from nature in that they prescribe the distinction between a correct and incorrect synthesis of any given kind of object. We can perform the former correctly even if we always perform the latter incorrectly. This is what marks the distinction. It is also what dissolves the contradiction to which *DA* is mistakenly meant as a remedy.[38]

6. The Dilemma Revisited

DA leaves the dilemma facing Kant's theory of perception where it was found. That dilemma, it will be remembered, goes like this. To be affected is to stand in some epistemic relation to an object. That object is either a thing in itself or a phenomenal object. If it is the former, we would be in direct epistemic contact with something which, on Kant's theory, we cannot have in our sensory fields. We would, in other words, obliterate the distinction between a phenomenal object and a thing as it is apart from what we perceive it to be. If the object affecting us is phenomenal, what is supposed to be called affection cannot be analyzed in terms of the relation in which an object stands to the forms of our sensibility. For the forms of our sensibility are, on Kant's theory, space and time. What makes an object phenomenal, on the same account, is the fact of spatio-temporal location. But in that case the notice of affection cannot be explicated in terms of the relation in which a *phenomenal* object stands to the forms of our sensibility. For such an object is already spatio-temporal and cannot, therefore, stand in the required relation to forms of sensibility like space and time.

The problem confronting the theory of double affection is really a problem which confronts the very notion of affection: There must be a justification for claiming that affection is an epistemic relation between an object and the forms of our sensibility while claiming at the same time that we cannot perceive things in themselves. But there would seem to be no hope in reconciling the two claims with each other. The problem is to find viable relata for the relation of affection. We have only two. And neither is viable. If you opt for things in themselves as the affecting agents, then you provide an object which cannot be perceived. And if you opt for phenomenal objects, you are left with the task of providing an object which cannot stand in the required relation to the forms of sensibility.

In either case, the appropriate relatum is missing. And this is not a problem that can be solved by contriving, in the tradition of Adickes, Vaihinger, and their Anglo-Saxon scions, a theory of double affection. The problems that beset Kant's theory of perception arise with single affection and, as I have tried to show, can only be duplicated by a corresponding duplication of affections.

The first step in removing the *prima facie* contradiction which vitiates the concept of affection is to reject a plausible but ultimately unsatisfactory solution. Suppose somebody claimed that space and time can be both the forms of our sensibility and the characteristics of the objects which we sensuously apprehend.[39] There is, it might be argued, nothing in the theory that space and time are the formal characteristics of our sensibility to imply that they cannot also inhere in the things we perceive. And this is obviously true. There is no contradiction. But even with this concession, the same problem which undoes *DA* in other precincts merely emerges all over again. The problem arises again with respect to the relation which the object we perceive has to its spatio-temporal characteristics. Even if we allow the possiblity that the objects we perceive have spatio-temporal characteristics, we do not rid ourselves of the issue with which we began. The issue concerns the relation between what we perceive and what Kant calls the forms of sensibility. The problem is reduplicated when those forms are also implanted in the things we perceive. Whatever problem that arises in the context of the objects we perceive and the forms under which we perceive them will merely arise all over again when the context is shifted to the objects we perceive and the spatio-temporal characteristics they have.

The upshot is that either the notion of a thing in itself must go from Kant's theory of perception or the notion of affection must be discarded. And this is a situation which *DA* is powerless to remedy. For the general strategy for applying *DA* must inevitably force the emergence of the original dilemma with respect to transcendent affection. Since we must make a distinction between what affects the sensibility of an ego in itself and what that object is in itself, we can raise all of the problems associated with affection within the context of a sensibility different from ours. And, what is equally disturbing for *DA*, to say that phenomenal objects affect the empirical ego raises the same problem with the fact that the affecting object is phenomenal that is raised about Kant's theory even without imputing *DA* to it. To say that space and time are forms under which we can be sensibly aware of any perceptual object does not prevent that object from satisfying spatio-temporal descriptions. But the problem about the proper description of the object which satisfies these descriptions does not disappear. To say that something is a form under which we must perceive an object if we are to experience it at all does not imply that the object which we experience lacks the properties which are designated as forms of perception. And such a claim is also completely silent about the relation between the objects we perceive and the characteristics they exemplify.

How, it remains to be shown, can we intuit things in themselves without contradicting the very notion of a thing in itself or, what is equally unsatisfactory for Kant's theory, transforming a thing in itself into a phenomenal object? The dilemma facing Kant's theory can be removed when we see that his notion of intuition admits a perception of things in themselves but that such an admission is harmless. Kant specifies the content of an intuition in a way that implies nothing about the spatio-temporal character of the object we are given. He gives us two criteria. We know something by intuition, in the first place, when we stand in an immediate epistemic relation to it.[40] And we intuit something, secondly, just in case that entity is singular or, equivalently, an individual rather than a common property.[41] What is important about these criteria for the present dilemma is that neither *implies* that a content of intuition is spatial or temporal. It may be the case that the individuals which are immediately presented to us also satisfy spatio-temporal descriptions; but nothing about the notion of immediacy or singularity as such requires them to do so.

The immediacy and singularity criteria do, however, imply that the objects we intuit are at best only contingently related to the spatial or temporal characteristics they might have. And it also follows that the singular entities which we may be given in intuition satisfy descriptions just insofar as they are singular; and this implies, further, that singular entities are logically independent of whatever spatial or temporal descriptions they may also satisfy. This tells us the sense in which we do intuit things in themselves when they affect our sensibility: We are immediately aware of individuals which satisfy descriptions which contain no spatial or temporal predicates. Thus the individuals we intuit may be presented with spatio-temporal characteristics; but when we intuit the individuals which are presented with spatial or temporal characteristics, what we intuit is not something that can be identified with those other entities. This is not to deny that spatial and temporal entities might also be individuals. Kant's argument in the Aesthetic in fact requires that spaces and times be kinds of individuals. For, as everybody knows, the account he gives of space there is that it is an infinite volume with other volumes contained within that volume to infinity. He believes, in other words, in the existence of a kind of particular he calls a volume.[42]

This belief extends to another kind of particular called a moment. This is the result of his application of the volume analogy to time.[43] Spaces and times must, on the present theory, be kinds of individuals. None of this, however, undermines the conclusions I have drawn from an examination of the singularity and immediacy criteria for intuitions. All it shows is that there are some kinds of particulars which have spatio-temporal characteristics essentially. This does not show that *all* individuals have spatio-temporal characteristics essentially. That moments and volumes have temporal or spatial characteristics essentially is, therefore, the logical result of their being spatial and temporal and not the consequence of their being singular items which are immediately given to us in intuition.

There is, if the foregoing argument is sound, a sense in which we do intuit things in themselves. But it is not a sense that would require the collapse of the distinction between a thing in itself and a phenomenal object. The latter is a particular together with the spatial or temporal characteristics which it must have if it is to be a perceptual object for us. But although the particular must be connected with space and time, the particular which affects us is not itself spatial or temporal. It is, at most, connected with a volume of space or a moment in time. This preserves the distinction between a phenomenal object and a thing in itself.[44] If the connection, say, between moments, spatial volumes, and the particulars occupying a spatial volume at a moment is contingent, then what we perceive when we are aware of a perceptual particular other than a moment or a spatial volume is an entity that can exist apart from the forms of our apprehension. This makes it a thing in itself. What makes it a phenomenal particular as well is its contingent relation to volumes and moments.

But there is a sense in which we cannot perceive things in themselves. Since the object we do perceive is only contingently connected to space and time, there is at least one possible world in which the particular could exist without satisfying any spatial or temporal description at all. Whatever properties it would have in such a world could not be perceived by us. This is compatible, however, with saying that the world in which we intuit the entity having spatio-temporal characteristics and the world in which other kinds of beings intuit the entity lacking such characteristics both contain the same *particular*.

Let me apply the distinctions for which I have been arguing to the solution of the dilemma raised by Kant's theory of perception. In the first place, things in themselves can affect us without becoming phenomenal objects. What affects us is the particular which satisfies the immediacy and singularity criteria for the content of a Kantian intuition. But a thing in itself does not affect us in the sense that the possible state of affairs of which the particular we intuit can be a part stands in no epistemic relation to us. This explains how it is possible to say that a thing in itself can be intuited without contradicting the very notion of a thing in itself. For, as I hope to have shown, that notion has two senses. We can call something a thing in itself just in case it is a particular which is only contingently related to the moments and spatial volumes which comprise our forms of perceptual awareness. Or we can call the very same particular a thing in itself when it is separated from moments and spatial volumes. The discrimination of these two senses of "thing in itself" allows an escape from the dilemma that could not have been provided by *DA*.

7. Residual Objections

The explication of the notion of affection which I have offered is bound to invite two plausible and initially powerful objections. Let me take them in turn.

1. The Objection from Transcendental Ideality

Some might still argue that my resolution of the dilemma ignores its most crucial objection. Space and time are, as Kant says, forms of our sensibility. They are nothing but the forms which, as Kant also says, lie a priori in the mind.[45] But if all of this is true, then somebody might contend that it is simply false to say that the particulars which we intuit satisfy spatio-temporal descriptions while still being things in themselves. Once you have said, in other words, that space and time are transcendentally ideal, then you have also said that they cannot attach to the particulars which we intuit.

The answer to this objection issues from a closer examination of Kant's argument to show that space and time are transcendentally ideal.[46] What Kant says is this. Space is not a property, relational or otherwise. He says, further, that this is equivalent to the claim that space is not "a determination which attaches to the objects themselves when abstraction has been made from all the subjective conditions of intuition."[47] Both of these claims are made to follow from this: If space were a characteristic of things in themselves rather than a subjective form of our apprehension, we would not be able to intuit it prior to the things which are in space.

What, exactly, does this argument prove? Kant's strategy here is to show that objects cannot have spatio-temporal characteristics because having them would be incompatible with our ability to intuit space prior to our acquaintance with objects in space. But the argument succeeds only on the assumption that space is to be construed as a relational or nonrelational *property*. If space were a property, we could not intuit it prior to the things which have it just because we cannot intuit a property that is uninstantiated. Consider, say, the relational property ". . . to the left of." If it were intuitable apart from the entities which instantiate it, it would have to be a singular which satisfies Kant's two criteria for an intuition. But the fact is that it is multiply instantiable. It cannot, therefore, be intuited as a singular entity satisfying Kant's criteria for an intuition. It assumes, accordingly, the simultaneous intuition of the entities instantiating spatial properties. But if space is a particular like a volume, then it would not be internally contradictory to maintain both that the particulars we intuit satisfy spatial descriptions and that space is transcendentally ideal in the sense that it is an a priori intuition constituting the condition of any object's being an object for us. Since space would, in this case, be a particular among particulars, our intuition of it would not be logically dependent upon intuiting the things to which it attaches. And this would be enough to show that objects could satisfy spatial descriptions even though space is transcendentally ideal.[48]

There is, I acknowledge, a troublesome addition to this line of reasoning. I refer to Kant's conclusion that whatever is an a priori intuition is not "a determination to the objects themselves, and which remains even when abstraction has been made of all the subjective conditions of intuition."[49] This would seem to commit us to the conclusion that the objects we intuit do not, after all, satisfy spatial descriptions. But all this claim states is that space is dependent for its existence upon the existence of acts of consciousness. And all this, in turn, shows us that space would cease to exist if acts of consciousness ceased to exist. It does not show that the objects in question fail to satisfy any spatial descriptions. It merely lays down a necessary condition under which such descriptions are true of objects; hence, the appeal to subjectivity does not buttress the objection from transcendental ideality.

2. The Objection from Phenomenal Properties

Someone might still argue, however, that the account I have given of the way in which we intuit things in themselves without doing irreparable damage to Kant's theory of perception succeeds only at the cost of impoverishing that theory completely. It can be maintained, so the objection might run, that the problem of numerical diversity has been solved but that the related issue of qualitative diversity has not been solved. When we perceive individuals, what we see are entities which, though they have spatio-temporal properties, do not have them essentially. But this is still silent about other features of a perceptual situatuion. There may be properties which perceptual individuals have that cannot be presented to us because of the peculiarities of our forms of intuition.

But this is only one part of the objection. It might also be argued that the problem of qualitative diversity serves only to raise the original dilemma facing Kant's theory all over again with respect to properties. Consider how this allegedly comes about. Distinguish between the spatio-temporal characteristics of things and such phenomenal characteristics as shape and size. If all we are allowed to introduce here is the property of spatiality, there is no way to account for the qualitative difference between, say, a square and a round shape in the spatial objects we intuit. But this demands that we add to the general notion of spatiality the phenomenal difference between different kinds of spatial characteristics. Yet such characteristics must, on Kant's theory, either be what I shall call properties in themselves or they must be manifestations of properties which cannot be intuited but which somehow act on our sensibility. Both alternatives cause difficulty for the theory. Take them in turn.

Suppose that the spatial properties are characteristics of what Kant calls things in themselves. This would disqualify them from counting as spatial or temporal. For it would be the same as saying that the properties in question are phenomenal. But suppose, for the sake of the argument, that they are phenomenal. This would seem to force us back to the alternative according to which the properties which we intuit are the result of the action of properties we do not intuit on our sensibility. And this would merely raise the problem confronting Kant's theory all over again. That problem arose because of an impossible set of conditions placed on the perception of objects. What we perceive must be a phenomenal object. Yet what is called a phenomenal object is the result of the action of a noumenal object on our sensibility. The former condition permits us to perceive things; but the latter condition prevents us from doing so just because it requires us to have the capacity to perceive things which we cannot perceive should we accept Kant's theory. The problem, it should be noticed, can be formulated in a perfectly general way without introducing the peculiarities of any specific kind of perceptual entity: It applies to perceptual individuals as well as perceptual properties. So far I have tried to solve the problem with respect to perceptual *individuals*. But it would seem that the same problem would arise all over again for perceptual *properties*.

But does it? I think not. Nothing in Kant's argument for the transcendental ideality of space implies a distinction between how the particulars we intuit are presently constituted in themselves and how they appear to us. As far as Kant's argument goes, we are required only to distinguish between how things are presently given to us and how they might be constituted in some other possible world. To explain how one spatial figure differs from another does not, in other words, demand that we make the distinction between properties of things in themselves and properties of objects as they appear to us. All it does demand, on Kant's theory of perception, is that we distinguish between the properties things have in the world which is presented to us and those properties which can be instantiated in the possible worlds with which we are not presented. And this is enough to escape the objection from phenomenal properties. For all it says is that we do not require the distinction between a property in itself and something called a phenomenal property in order to account for the fact of qualitative diversity. We do not need such a distinction; but this does not imply a lack of need for a distinction between things in themselves and things as they are presented to us. The Objection from Phenomenal Properties does not, therefore, force us to make the impossible distinction between properties in themselves and phenomenal properties.

Before relegating *DA* to philosophy's population of theoretical myths, let me take stock of why it fails and why what it purports to accomplish can be done without its dubious aid. It fails both exegetically and philosophically. The former failure can be traced to the fact that the doctrines to which *DA* theorists appeal are compatible with other, quite different, theories of affection. The latter failure can be found in the fact that the theory which *DA* attributes to Kant merely duplicates the problems it is supposed to solve. In neither case does the dilemma facing that theory demand or profit from the introduction of two kinds of affection. The proper solution must, I conclude, rely on a different interpretation of the notion of a perceptual individual and its relation to a thing in itself. And this, in turn, demands an interpretation of the relation of individuation to our sensibility very different from the one on which *DA* is based. Once such an interpretation has been given, the problem raised by the dilemma originally facing Kant's theory disappears.

NOTES

1. *Critique of Pure Reason,* A20/B34. (All unspecified references in the sequel are to the foregoing work.) The major statement of double affection is in Erich Adickes, *Kants Lehre von der doppelten Affektion unseres Ich* (Tübingen: J. C. B. Mohr, 1929), pp. 27-59 and pp. 32ff. (Hereinafter cited as KL.) Cf. Herbert Herring, *Das Problem der Affektion bei Kant, Kant-Studien,* Ergänzungsheft 67 (Köln, Kolns Universitätsverlag, 1953), for a review of the history of the problem. Cf. also Hans Vaihinger, *Commentar zu Kant's 'Kritik der reinen Vernunft'* (Leipzig; Union Deutsche Verlagsgesellschaft, 1892), for a review of the sources out of which the theory of double affection grew. (Hereinafter cited as CZ.) See T. D. Weldon, *Kant's 'Critique of Pure Reason'* (Oxford: The Clarendon Press, 1958), pp. 252-56, and Norman Kemp Smith, *A Commentary to Kant's 'Critique of Pure Reason'* (New York: Humanities Press, 1962), Appendix C, for brief English summaries of the Adickes view. I consciously restrict my discussion of *DA* to the first *Kritik.* I do this despite the claim of Norman Kemp Smith, *Commentary,* p. 614, that the *Opus postumum* is the place at which *DA* emerges in its most explicit form. What distinguishes Kant's view in the first *Kritik* from his view in the *Opus postumum* is primarily a thesis in the latter concerning the productivity of the ego. Thus in the *Opus postumum* Kant claims that the thing in itself is "the mere representation of the self's activity" [cited by Erich Adickes, *Kant's 'Opus postumum', dargestellt und beurteilt* (Berlin: 1920), p. 654]. This marks a distinction between the two works; but it does not mark an advanced form of *DA* for the simple reason that *DA* assumes a relation of affection and such a relation cannot obtain if one of the ostensible terms of that relation is a product of the other term. The theory to be found in the *Opus postumum* is not, I conclude, relevant to the assessment of the quite

different theory which adherents of *DA* allege is to be found in the first *Kritik*. Significantly, where the two theories do agree, Adickes cites the argument from the first *Kritik*. If the basis for *DA* in the first *Kritik* can be disqualified, the corresponding passages in the *Opus postumum* will also be disqualified. Cf. Norman Kemp Smith, *Commentary*, pp. 625ff, for a comprehensive list of references to the peculiarity of the *Opus postumum* theory.

2. Kant says that things in themselves are the primary sources of sensible experience at A538/B566, A540/B568, A557/B585, A564/B594, A565-6/B593-4, and A613/B641-2.

3. Cf. Norman Kemp Smith, *Commentary*, pp. 217-18, 275ff for an enumeration and discussion of the relevant passages.

4. A19/B33.

5. A19/B33; cf. A493/B522. For a critical assessment of this alternative see Henry E. Allison, *The Kant-Eberhard Controversy* (Baltimore: The Johns Hopkins University Press, 1973), pp. 29ff.

6. I follow here the statement of *DA* given by Erich Adickes in KL. Hans Vaihinger in CZ, 2: 35-55, gives a similar formulation. For a good summary of Vaihinger, see Anton Thomsen, "Bemerkungen zur Kritik des Kantischen Begriffes des Dinges an sich," *Kant-Studien* 8: 254ff.

7. Cf. Adickes, KL, p. 14. The textual basis for the coinage "appearance in itself" is A28-29/B44-45. The defense of such a notion is in Adickes, KL, pp. 22ff, especially p. 22: "Die räumliche Aussenwelt ist also zwar Erscheinung, aber nicht eine solche des empirischen Ich; ihm ist sie vielmehr gleichgestellt, steht ihm selbstständig und unabhängig gegenüber, wird nicht von ihm produziert, sondern (als eine vom Ich an sich geschaffene) vorgefunden, besitzt also im Verhältnis zu ihm eine Art von An-sich-Charakter."

8. The terms "empirical affection" and "transcendent affection" are Vaihinger's but are also used by Adickes, KL, p. 4. Erich Adickes, KL, p. 22ff, puts it as follows: (i) the empirical ego generates empirical representations because it is affected by spatial objects; (ii) but these objects are also appearances; and (iii) they are produced *(geschaffen)* by the ego in itself; (iv) appearances exist in themselves *(an sich)* for the empirical ego but are mere appearances *(blosse Erscheinungen)* for the ego in itself; and (v) the result of empirical affection is sensation *(Empfindung)*.

9. Cf. Adickes, KL, p. 22 and Vaihinger, CZ, 1: 35.

10. What follows is a summary of Adickes, KL, p. 35. The theory has not died out. More recently Wilfrid Sellars in his *Science and Metaphysics* (New York: Humanities Press, 1968) has endorsed it. Cf. especially p. 52: "The doctrine of 'double affection' is an essential feature of Kant's thought. Correctly understood, it simply tells us that the

transcendentally conceived non-spatial, non-temporal action of the non-ego on human receptivity, generating the manifold of sense (which action is required to explain how the *esse* of the experienced world can be *concipi* and yet non-arbitrary and inter-subjective) has as its counterpart in the represent*ed* world the action of material things on our sense organs and, through them on the sensory faculties of the empirical self."

11. For this distinction see especially the *Opus postumum* AA 22, 339, 363-5.

12. A28/B45.

13. B307.

14. I am aware that Kant has more than one way of distinguishing between sensuous and nonsensuous faculties of intuition. One such way apparently diverges from the claim I make about the implications of the inevitability of some kind of account of the distinction between our acquaintance with particulars and our acquaintance with concepts. Thus as early as *De mundi sensibilis atque intelligibilis forma et pricnipiis,* §10, he claims that the distinction between these two kinds of apprehension would not apply to a being with non-sensuous intuition. The same claim runs through Kant's entire development. It emerges again in a letter to Marcus Herz dated 21 February 1772 (AA 8, 689). Passages like these do not disconfirm my claim that we must be able to make the distinction between sensibility and intellect even with respect to beings that have nonsensuous forms of intuition. All that it requires is the distinction between beings lacking any faculty of intuition at all and those which have a faculty of intuition with characteristics unlike ours.

15. Cf. *Prolegomena,* §13, n.II; A28/B44; A358ff. Other passages containing what purports to be discussion of empirical affection are *De mundi sensibilis atque intelligibilis forma et principiis,* §3, §4, and §15A; cf. also *Reflexion* 4972. Adickes, KL, p. 13 n.1, gives an extensive list of similar passages in the *Opus postumum.* But if my argument is correct, none of them establishes the existence of two kinds of affection.

16. A45/B63–A46/B64; cf. A232/B285, A257/B313, A393. Adickes, KL, p. 35, cites this as a case of implied empirical affection without distinguishing it from the rose example.

17. Cf. my "Causation and Direct Realism," *The Philosophy of Science* 39 (1972): 388-96.

18. P. F. Strawson, *The Bounds of Sense* (London: Methuen and Co. Ltd., 1966), pp. 41ff, exemplies the confusion of causation and affection. He claims, for example (p.41), that for Kant a thing in itself is what science tells us is the constitution of nature, whereas phenomenal

objects are the result of the causal action of entities so constituted on our sensory apparatus. Strawson rightly objects that such a doctrine is intelligible only so long as we think of the thing which affects us as being spatio-temporal. Without this provision, the notion of affection is, I agree, meaningless. What goes wrong with the Strawsonian criticism, however, is that it falsely assumes affection to be a kind of causation. It thereby fails to lay bare the real relation between things in themselves and the forms of intuition in affection. A similar mistake is to be found in Jonathan Bennett, *Kant's Analytic* (Cambridge: The University Press, 1966), pp. 19ff. For a more extended discussion of this issue set in a different context, see my "Causation and Direct Realism," *The Philosophy of Science* 39 (1972): 388-96.

19. A28/B44; *Prolegomena,* § 13.
20. Adickes, KL, pp.67-74.
21. A28/B44 and A36/B52.
22. A26/B42ff; A333/B49ff. Cf. A36/B53 and A44/B62ff.
23. Cf. Adickes, KL, p. 69, where he claims that for Kant "die Subjektivität der sekundären Sinnesqualitäten einen ganz anderen Ursprung hat als die Idealität von Raum und Zeit: hier kommt die geistige Organisation des Ich an sich, dort die des empirischen Ich als Quelle in Betracht. . . ."
24. Cf. Adickes, KL, p. 69.
25. The major passages here are A28/B44ff., A29, and *Prolegomena,* § 13. Cf. also Hans Vaihinger, CZ, 2: 363ff. For the classical statements of the primary-secondary distinction, see John Locke, *Essay Concerning Human Understanding,* Book II, Chapter 8, and George Berkeley, *Principles of Human Knowledge,* Sections 9-20. The most thorough recent discussion of the distinction is given by Reginald Jackson, "Locke's Distinction Between Primary and Secondary Qualities," *Mind* 38 (1921): 56-76, reprinted in C. B. Martin and D. M. Armstrong, editors, *Locke and Berkeley* (Garden City, New York: Anchor Books, 1968), pp. 53-77.
26. Cf. Adickes, KL, pp. 74ff; Vaihinger, CZ, 2: 180.
27. A431/B459. Cf. *Metaphysische Anfangsgründe der Naturwissenschaft* (AA 4, 510), translated into English by James Ellington (Indianapolis: The Bobbs-Merrill Company, 1970), pp. 58-59.
28. Cf. *De mundi sensibilis atque intelligibilis forma et principiis,* § 4, § 16, § 22, and § 27. See also Erich Adickes, *Kant und das Ding an Sich* (Berlin: Pan Verlag Rolf Heise, 1924), pp. 7, 12, and 28.
29. Cf. Adickes, KL, pp. 78-79.
30. Cf. A251, A538/B566, A566/B594; *Prolegomena,* § 32, § 57. Cf. Also Erich Adickes, *Kant und das Ding an Sich* pp. 4ff.
31. Cf. Erich Adickes, KL, pp. 81ff.

32. A127ff, B165.
33. For Kant's definition of "affinity," see A113. Cf. A122 and A600/B628.
34. B164, A125, A127, and B134ff.
35. Cf. Erich Adickes, KL, pp. 84ff.
36. Cf. Erich Adickes, KL, pp. 91ff.
37. Cf. Erich Adickes, KL, p. 91.
38. For a discussion of this issue in a wider context, see my *Kant, Ontology, and the A Priori* (Evanston: Northwestern University Press, 1968), Chapter 5, passim. For further discussion of the distinction between general and particular rules of synthesis, see my "Must Transcendental Arguments be Spurious?" forthcoming in *Kant-Studien.*
39. The suggestion I consider here was first made by Trendelenburg and led to the famous Trendelenburg-Fischer controversy. For a good description of the course of that controversy, see Vaihinger, CZ, 2, pp. 134ff.
40. A19/B34. Cf. also A320/B376 and *Prolegomena*, §8. In his "Kant's Philosophy of Arithmetic," in *Philosophy, Science, and Method* (New York: St. Martin's Press, 1969), Sidney Morgenbesser et al., ed., Charles Parsons has stated this and the following criterion in some detail. Manley Thompson, "Singular Terms and Intuitions in Kant's Epistemology," *The Review of Metaphysics* 26 (1972): 332 adds what he calls a uniqueness condition to the application of terms denoting the contents of intuition. I consciously ignore this because, even if the criteria for application of "intuition" were to be supplemented in this way, nothing follows about the necessary spatio-temporality of what is uniquely designated.
41. Cf. A25/B39.
42. Cf. A25/B39.
43. Cf. A32/B47ff.
44. For a discussion of this issue in a broader context, see my article, in two parts, "How to Dispense with Things in Themselves," forthcoming in *Ratio.*
45. A41/B52.
46. A38/B54.
47. A26/B42.
48. Cf. Edwin B. Allaire, "Existence, Independence, and Universals," *The Philosophical Review* 69 (1960): 485-496, reprinted in *Essays in Ontology* (The Hague: Martinus Nijhoff, 1963), pp. 3-13, for a discussion of this kind of dependence.
49. Ibid.

THE CONSTITUTIVE ROLE OF PRACTICAL REASON IN KANT'S MORAL PHILOSOPHY

George Schrader

If ethics is to be taken at all seriously it is impossible to separate normative from descriptive considerations. Not only must any descriptive account of human existence be compatible with the prescriptions of ethical theory, but ethical theory must contribute to the descriptive analysis. Unless it is willing to speak only of a hypothetical or fictional being, ethics must describe man as a moral agent. It must consider how he can have ideal aspirations and show why certain aspirations are more valid than others. That job simply cannot be done by considering the values themselves, since it is their validity for man that is in question. Similarly, it must show how man is actually obligated. Moreover, if choice is to be allowed, freedom must be shown to be a fact rather than a possibility.

The objection might be offered at this point that although ethical prescriptions must somehow be related to human actuality, this task does not fall to ethics. Ethics is not concerned about the way in which men behave but in the way in which they *ought* to behave. The problem of showing how ethical considerations might influence human behavior thus falls to philosophical psychology and the social sciences rather than to ethics. One might thus agree with Kant that duty can be clearly specified even though no man may ever have honored it. If viewed in this way, "practical anthropology," as Kant termed it, is ancillary to rather than a component of ethical theory. The difficulty with this resolution of the problem is that it refers the question to a third party but without conveying the necessary authority to settle differences. Kant clearly did not intend that practical anthropology should modify the canons of duty to fit the fact of human nature. On the contrary, anthropology was presumably required to accommodate human nature to the requirements of ethics as best it could. It never occurred to Kant that the analysis of human nature at the empirical level might cast serious doubt on his ethical theory. Yet, as we shall have occasion to see, his own account of empirical motivation was far from satisfactory.

The point I wish to make, however, is that any dispute between two autonomous disciplines can be adjudicated only by a supervening authority. If it is the same being who acts both morally and from empirical motivations, some account must be given of the way in which the two halves fit together. We need, in other words, a philosophical theory of human nature that is authorized to reconcile and integrate the empirical and moral components. To represent man in his totality such a theory must be allowed to make whatever adjustments are necessary in the empirical and the moral conceptions of man. It must be in a position to examine the assumptions, data, and conclusions of each perspective. Honoring the integrity of each perspective, it must provide a more inclusive context within which empirical and ethical motivations can be more satisfactorily understood. Although it cannot sweep aside either the empirical or the ethical study of the human situation, it must question each of them and thus participate actively in both lines of inquiry. We need not only an ethical understanding of human motivation but a philosophical understanding of ethics.

Kant is a pivotal figure for modern ethical theory in that he both refused to base his ethics on an empirical analysis of human behavior and, yet, related this ethical theory to a comprehensive theory of man. Our earlier reference to Kant might

thus have been misleading in suggesting that he dispensed altogether with a theory of human nature. On the contrary, Kant
insisted on a metaphysical context for the consideration of
ethical principles. His metaphysics of morals was essentially a
metaphysics of human existence developed from a moral or
what he termed "practical" point of view. Thus Kant took duty
to be a fact of human existence, the crucial fact for the
development of an ethical theory. Moreover, he considered the
fact of duty to provide a sufficient proof of the reality of
human freedom. He recognized explicitly, therefore, that his
ethical theory had descriptive import. Because he assigned priority to "practical reason" he regarded the ethical description of
the human situation as more fundamental than any empirical
analysis. To paraphrase one of Kant's own statements, his
analysis of human nature was designed to make room for
human freedom. As Kant recognized, without freedom ethics
would be illusory. The fact that practical anthropology can be
worked out independently does not mean, therefore, that ethics
can dispense with a descriptive account of human existence. On
the contrary, the metaphysics of morals must provide the guide-
lines and supply the categories for the empirical analysis of
human motivation. Practical anthropology must thus be developed from the standpoint of practical rather than pure theoretical reason. Its task is to fill in the outline of a theory of
existence rather than to supply an independent analysis.

Accounts of Kant's ethics have frequently assumed that all
empirical processes fall within experience as analyzed in the
Critique of Pure Reason. Carrying the distinction between *phenomena* and *noumena* over into the *Critique of Practical Reason*
they have looked upon the moral law as relating to empirical
processes that are causally ordered. When viewed in this light,
the problem of applying the categorical imperative to human
action is just as difficult as many of his critics have maintained.
Indeed, it is impossible. The fact is, however, that the distinction between phenomena and noumena has no more place
within moral experience than it has within cognitive experience.
The analysis of empirical cognition does not make use of the
distinction between appearances and things in themselves. The
fundamental distinction within cognitive experience is that between the sensible and the conceptual or, as Kant frequently

states it, the empirical and the transcendental. It is only when we consider the limits of experience that the distinction between phenomena and noumena is either necessary or meaningful. The situation is very much the same in the case of morality. The tension there, as in the case of cognition, is between empirical motivations (inclinations) and the demands of pure practical reason. We are dealing with a different world from top to bottom when we analyze experience from the perspective of morality. It is now seen from the situation of man as agent and actor rather than as observer. And this means that man sees himself quite differently with respect to every detail of his experience.

Even a cursory look at the language Kant uses in referring to the empirical data of ethics should settle this point. The generic term Kant uses to designate empirical processes provides the key. He designates those empirical processes which are relevant for ethical analysis as "inclinations." But he is careful to specify that an inclination is both conscious and telic. As he defines it in his *Lectures on Anthropology,* an inclination is the habitual desire for an object through the representation of it as an end. To understand what an inclination is we must understand what it intends and thus view it from the perspective of the agent. An inclination could not in principle be subsumed under the category of causality as specified in the first *Critique.* It could neither be observed nor included within the manifold of sensibility. In the Aesthetic of the first *Critique* Kant had expressly excluded both feeling and volition. Since inclination is a manifestation of desire and falls under those categories which pertain to volition, it could not be considered among the data of the phenomenal world. This does not entail, however, that it must be ascribed to noumena, but only that it can be analyzed from an alternative perspective. It is not just the rational will that cannot be included within the phenomenal world but the whole range of empirical inclinations and desires. In several places Kant refers to Practical Reason as "the faculty of desire." It is apparent that he conceived of Practical Reason as encompassing the whole gamut of moral experience from appetition to the pure rational will. The problem of applying the moral law to human action is far less difficult if one views it as pertaining to empirical desires which are both conscious and intentional. One may then view the pure rational will as related to empirical motivations in much the same way as the understanding is related to sensibility. To be coherent, Kant's ethical theory requires a "transcendental unity of volition" which corresponds to the "transcendental unity of apperception" of the first *Critique.*

Kant regarded happiness as the inclusive end of empirical desire, yet happiness could not possibly be a datum for cognitive analysis in the phenomenal world. Kant defines happiness as the fulfillment of human desire. Moreover, he insists that reason is instrumental in the definition of happiness as an end. Since the quest for happiness is oriented toward a final end, it cannot be analyzed causally.

However we may experience happiness, it is *not* through sensible intuition as characterized in the Aesthetic of the first *Critique.* Even psychology, if it were developed in conformity with the principles of pure theoretical reason, would have nothing to say about happiness, for the simple reason that it could know nothing about it. If inclination and happiness are empirical phenomena, they must be assigned to the domain of practical reason and, hence, to morality rather than to theoretical reason. It is thus completely mistaken to view Kant's normative ethics as based upon an objective theory of human behavior structured by the categories of pure theoretical reason. No ethics could have such a foundation and if Kant had predicated his normative ethics on such a basis he would have been utterly defenseless before his critics.

Kant was a pivotal figure because, on the one hand, he refused to derive normative conclusions from a scientific description of the phenomenal world. In separating ethics completely from science he severed the connection between the descriptive "is" and the normative "ought." In this respect he anticipated the formulation of the "naturalistic fallacy" and avoided it. But there was another side to Kant's ethics which made it possible for G. E. Moore to accuse him of committing the fallacy. For even though Kant did not appeal to a scientific theory of man to validate and support his ethics, he made use of a descriptive account of human nature, nonetheless, and could thus be accused of deriving normative conclusions from an analysis of matters of fact. The question is, however, whether this is a fallacy at all. Moore assumed that matters of fact have no normative import and he thus considered empirical facts in much the same way as had Kant in the *Critique of Pure Reason*. Freedom, however, is a curious kind of fact and cannot be fitted into the phenomenal realm as Kant had conceived of it. But it does fit into the moral order and can be both analyzed and described from a practical point of view. Kant's ethical theory thus points beyond Moore to another perspective on the value/fact issue. If Kant is correct in his conviction that primacy must be assigned to practical reason and if practical reason can validate norms through a descriptive analysis of the human situation, the descriptive/normative issue can be bypassed. In his 'metaphysics of morals' Kant prepared the way for a descriptive account of human existence which could include the ethical within the scope of its investigation. It is this direction that has been pursued by Hegel, Kierkegaard, and the existentialist philosophers generally.

It is unfortunate that in his *Critique of Practical Reason* Kant did not provide an Aesthetic. His account of the moral will lacks the kind of careful and detailed analysis of empirical motivation that had been supplied for sensible intuition in the *Critique of Pure Reason*. It is possible to supply the essential components of an Aesthetic of Practical Reason, but to do so one must collect materials from a variety of Kant's essays. The lack of an Aesthetic is doubly unfortunate, however, in that some of Kant's assumptions about empirical motivation are open to serious question. It is not enough, I believe, to supply the missing Aesthetic. It is necessary, also, to modify it to make it accord both with the facts of human experience and the requirements of Kant's normative ethics. Even though Kant did not base his ethics on an objective empirical account of human motivation, he carried over some basic assumptions from his analysis of cognition. His epistemology and his ethics thus have in common several important features—though not the one feature which is most commonly alluded to, namely, that the empirical is the phenomenal. Since these assumptions have been widely shared by contemporary moralists, they merit careful examination.

The main problem of Kant's first *Critique*—and in many ways the central problem of modern epistemology—concerns the relationship between sensation and conceptual thought. Kant was persuaded, as have been the majority of post-Kantian philosophers, that all material for empirical cognition comes from sensation. At the same time, however, he recognized that objective knowledge requires the organization of sensible data. As an empiricist he was anxious to preserve the autonomy of sensation to the fullest extent possible. As a proponent of science, on the other hand, he was eager to demonstrate that sensible data are amenable to the forms of conceptual thought. The problem was to show how two such alien factors can be combined to provide us with empirical knowledge. Stated in the simplest possible terms, Kant's solution to this problem consisted in the demonstration that all empirical awareness is subject to transcendental rules. Since there is ultimately only one consciousness, our awareness at any level must accede to those conditions which are necessary for the unity of self-consciousness. It follows, therefore, that although sensation is relatively autonomous in that, within limits, it follows its own contingent rules, to be possible at all it must conform to those higher (conceptual) conditions which provide the necessary structural unity of our experience. As Kant worked out the subtle argument of the Analytic and, particularly, the Deduction of Categories, he found it necessary to specify an increasingly complex set of conditions for sensibility. We discover that the understanding can organize sensible data conceptually only because it has had at least a minimal role in their original apprehension.

If the problem of Kant's epistemology is to explain how reason can structure sensible intuition to provide knowledge of objects, the problem of his ethics is to show how reason can regulate the empirical will. The problem is not given the same prominence in the *Critique of Practical Reason* as in his first *Critique,* but it is no less acute. To show that reason can be practical—one of the main tasks of Kant's ethics—it must be established that reason can govern inclinations and control action. To ask how practical reason can influence the empirical will is thus like asking how the understanding can order sensible intuition. In both cases the ordering faculty is external to the data which it is required to regulate. How then can the moral law be legislative in fact as well as in theory?

Kant has an answer and, I believe, a perfectly satisfactory answer to this question. But I am not at all sure that the answer he ultimately gives is fully consistent with his anthropological theory. The resolution of the problem requires the unity of a will which operates at the level both of inclination and pure rational volition. Practical reason can be legislative for human action only because there is one will which informs empirical desire, issues, and the moral imperative. In the Deduction of the first *Critique* Kant had argued that sensible intuition can provide materials for judgment only because they are both "accompanied by the 'I think'." This is a somewhat awkward statement, but its meaning is clear enough. I can make use of sensations in my judgments only because it is one and the same consciousness (my own) which animates the two acts. Sensible intuition cannot, therefore, be blind. In his ethical writings Kant refers to the will as standing midway between its empirical and a priori manifestations—in other words, as underlying both of them and, hence, as encompassing the entire faculty of desire. Sometimes he uses different terms *(Wille* and *Willkür)* to designate the two aspects of volition. It would be quite mistaken, however, to regard these as two separate faculties, the one empirical and the other rational. They are rather different capacities of the same will or, in Kant's terminology, "faculty of desire." The two component features of volition-empirical desire and the prescription of rational law—can thus be reconciled with one another because they are but relatively distinct expressions of a basically unitary will. This is the basic form of a "deduction" of the principles of the Pure Practical Reason. It is, I believe, sound in theory and can be justified in application. If Kant had stated it more explicitly and given it more prominence in his ethical writings, his readers would have been far less troubled about the applicability of the moral law.

In its most inclusive meaning, therefore, practical reason comprehends both empirical desire and the rationally informed will. Reason is required not only for the definition of happiness but for the constitution of inclination—though Kant never analyzed the latter function in any detail. Since inclinations are both conscious, purposive, and involve always the representation of the objects to which the inclinations refer, they must obviously be subsumed under the categories of volition. Hence, they fall within what Kant termed the sphere of freedom rather than nature. Freedom is a fact of practical reason and an encompassing fact. When viewed from the perspective of the agent, man is seen to be an autonomous being. He is autonomous not only by virtue of his capacity to subject his volition to a rational law, but also because even his most unreflective behavior manifests some degree of purposiveness. No matter how he acts, man gives a law of some sort to his activity and his world. To the degree that he determines his will reflectively in accord with the moral law he makes his autonomy the supreme princple of his action. No man can fail to be morally accountable since none can escape the demands of his own reason. Yet, this does not entail that we must live responsibly in the normative sense of that term. Although we are free and autonomous beings for whom reason is an indispensable faculty, we may refuse to make our autonomy the principle of our volition and thus refuse to honor the moral law in our action. Since the moral law is the law of our own freedom, to repudiate the law is to negate the autonomy which is constitutive of our nature as moral beings. In the last analysis it is our nature as persons and, hence, as human beings that is negated by the repudiation of the moral law. The moral imperative is thus obligatory in two senses: it is the supreme norm of human action and hence an ideal ought; but it is, also, the animating principle of our freedom and, hence, a necessary condition of our action. It is only because the moral law is anchored in our existence as self-determining agents that it can be expressed as a "categorical imperative." It is evident, therefore, that apart from his descriptive account of man as a being whose consciousness and volition permeate his every activity, Kant would have been unable to justify the moral law as a principle of freedom. It is not too much to say, perhaps, that Kant's ethical theory is nothing more than a descriptive account of human existence. If the moral law is normatively valid then it must be *in fact* a condition of human freedom.

Kant's readers have differed widely in the way they have interpreted his ethical theory. In suggesting the form which the "deduction" of ethical principles takes in his ethical writings I have emphasized one strand in his theory. There is another and somewhat different strand which stands in tension if not opposition to such a unitary theory of volition. Before we turn to the consideration of the more dualistic tendency in his moral philosophy it is important to note, however, that there can hardly be dispute about some of his most basic ethical doctrines. It is perfectly evident, in the first place, that freedom and autonomy serve both as normative and descriptive concepts in his ethical writings. It is equally apparent that he regarded volition as both empirical and reflective and, thus, as the factor which mediates between inclination and pure practical reason. Thirdly, he expressly referred to the "faculty of desire" as the province of practical reason. However we interpret him, I see no way in which his descriptive categories can be divorced from his normative principles.

In spite of the unity of the will which is presupposed in Kant's ethical theory, the same problem occurs with respect to sensible and rational components as in his theory of cognition. If, in the first *Critique,* the issue was: How can sensible intuition be regulated by the understanding?; in the second *Critique* it takes the form: How can empirical desire be governed by the rational will? In both cases the problem arises because of the autonomy of sensation and inclination. Neither sensible intuition nor inclination is blind; both exhibit intrinsic rational form of some sort.

Yet, they are *sui generis* and follow their own contingent laws. Since they are not internally constituted by the understanding or by reason, they must be structured and controlled by a higher faculty which imposes its rules upon them. Although they have only a limited autonomy in that they can be conceptually disciplined, they are not affected in their intrinsic nature by such basically alien forms. The question is, then, how the possibility of an external regulation of empirical processes can be guaranteed.

Kant made no attempt to investigate empirical motivation systematically. Although he lectured on the topic, he did not regard his observations as anything more than empirical generalizations. He assumed, however, that inclinations are not only contingent but highly variable. Moreover, he considered them to be no more subject to direct rational control than sensation itself. Men differ widely in temperament as in disposition. Some men are naturally sociable and others shy and retiring. Some take spontaneous delight in benevolent actions whereas others manifest no natural concern for their fellow men. It was, in fact, the highly contingent and variable nature of man as an empirical being that prompted Kant to place so much stress on the universality of the rational will. We cannot, if we are at all realistic about human nature, expect that all men will show consideration for their neighbors from a kindly natural disposition. Any such belief must be dismissed as romatically sentimental. Yet every man can, through the exercise of his rational will, treat his neighbor with respect—no matter how he may naturally feel toward him. Kant recognized that some men are blessed with a temperament which makes it relatively easy for them to abide by the canons of morality, whereas for others it is a struggle. We may lament the temperament which we have received from what Kant termed a "stepmotherly" nature, but we can do our duty nonetheless. Normative ethics is concerned about the variable patterns of man's empirically determined character only in so far as they provide materials for moral legislation. The contingent empirical order can be modified through moral volition to conform to the demands of the moral law. The moral order is achieved in the individual or the society by the exercise of a constraining power. It should be noted, however, that the regulative will does not and cannot supplant the intrinsic ends of empirical desire; it can only render them subservient to the sometimes alien ends of moral volition. There can in principle be no guarantee that we will spontaneously desire those ends which we are obligated to seek. The morally determined consciousness is frequently, though not of necessity, an alienated or what Hegel termed an "unhappy consciousness."

Still, the disparity between inclination and duty in Kant's ethics should not be overdrawn. It is not the case, as some of his critics have averred, that moral volition requires an opposition between them. On the contrary, our inclinations often support that which duty requires. Indeed, Kant held that we have a direct duty to promote the happiness of others and an indirect duty to promote our own happiness precisely because happiness is conducive to the pursuit of moral duty. He was not so much a pessimist as a realist so far as everyday human motivation is concerned. However rigorous his ethics may appear to be, it is a commonplace fact that we must often displace our immediate desires if we are to do that which is morally required of us. This much of Kant's analysis must surely be accepted as corresponding to the facts of our everyday experience. But we are confronted with two further questions the answer to which is not so apparent. Are we in no way morally accountable for our inclinations themselves? Suppose that we are tempted to violate our duty, for example by shortchanging someone for the sake of our own profit. Can this "temptation" be analyzed simply as a natural tendency to satisfy a nonmoral desire? In other words are our initial inclinations and desires, our temperament and our empirical character, properly to be regarded as morally neutral? In considering this question Kant stated that it is not for the inclinations themselves but for the consent we give to them that we are morally blameworthy. Does this mean, then, that the temptation to cheat is not itself morally blameworthy but only the volition which assents to that action in the face of a contrary duty?

Does this mean that the moral temptation is whether to cheat or not to cheat the other person? This is, in fact, an example which Kant uses to illustrate the kind of conflict that may occur between duty and inclination. As he analyzes it, there is a maxim involved in electing to cheat one's customer. The maxim which is presupposed in a dishonest action fails to conform to the demands of the moral law and must be rejected on moral grounds. The critical issue that is involved here is precisely how the maxim enters into the immoral action. In which of two ways are we to analyze what is involved in cheating someone? Shall we say: (a) that a particular individual happened to have quite natural but morally unfortunate tendencies to advance his own material profit at the expense of others; that this tendency, taken by itself, is neither morally good nor evil—indeed that it is not a morally accountable disposition at all; that such a tendency becomes morally significant only when it is consented to by the will and thus countermands the imperative of morality? If we analyze it in this fashion it would be misleading to refer to the tendency to advance one's profit at the expense of others as "cheating" since the latter term carries explicit moral overtones and implies the intention to take advantage of another person. Or, (b) as an alternative, shall we analyze the situation in a quite different way to assert: that the tendency to deliver to a customer less than he expects and has tacitly been promised reflects an intention both to deceive the customer and to use him simply as a means for one's own profit; that it is far from innocent of morally significant motivations; and, finally, that it reflects a morally bad will not simply in the consent to the action but in the constitution of the action itself?

Kant would, I believe, have analyzed the situation in the first rather than in the second way and thus would not have regarded the storekeeper as morally culpable for his desire to cheat his customer—so long as it was not consented to by his will. Moreover, Kant would have given him full moral credit so long as he resisted the temptation to cheat his customer—even though he secretly retained that desire. The distinction between the natural tendency to take advantage of someone and the deliberate intent to do so is thus crucially important for Kant's analysis. The moral maxim must not be confused with the intention of the natural inclination, else we blame the man for something that he has not willed and, presumably, could not avoid. I wonder, though, if at this point Kant is actually rigorous enough? Are our natural dispositions really so innocent as his analysis assumes? Can we actually make such a neat separation between the intention that informs a natural inclination and that which is expressed in the maxim of our moral volition?

If Kant had inspected his example a bit more closely he might well have found good reason for modifying his analysis somewhat. If we take Kant's hypothetical case of a storekeeper who is tempted to cheat a child, we must assume that the storekeeper contemplated a dishonest action and one that would knowingly exploit another person. As Kant explicitly declared, even the simplest inclination entertains a representation of its object. So complex a motivation as that of the dishonest storekeeper could hardly be devoid of intentional structure. It is not conceivable that he could seek to deceive and exploit the child without intending to do so. Hence, there must be a moral maxim that is intrinsic to his action. It is not accurate therefore to analyze the "temptation" as the weighing of a morally neutral line of action against a possible moral intention. In such a situation we do not ask ourselves: What maxim would this sort of action have if morally willed? On the contrary, we inspect the moral intention that is required for the very possibility of the action. Moral reflection does not in and of itself constitute such actions as cheating, lying, and deceiving. They are already so constituted by the will which informs and posits them. To say, then, that morally wrong action results from our "consent" to inclination will not, in this kind of case at least, suffice as a description of the motivation involved.

In his use of the doctrine of consent Kant was attempting to soften the incipient dualism of his theory of motivation. Recognizing that no man could be judged morally evil for his inclinations themselves—since on his theory they are natural dispositions—he limited moral responsibility to the consent we give or fail to give to them. There are, however, several difficulties in this way of trying to relate moral volition to impulse and inclination. In the first place it does not, as we have seen, take account of those intentions which are necessary for the constitution of the action to be judged. Deception, for example, cannot be analyzed as the natural and morally innocent disposition to misrepresent something to another person *plus* a moral intention to violate the categorical imperative. If there is anything morally wrong about deceiving others it must reside in the concrete act of deception itself. The moral maxim must, therefore, be constitutive of rather than external to the action. Even if we assume that deception may be carried out without deliberation and, hence, without reflecting on the ultimate principles involved, it still cannot be viewed as morally innocent or neutral. No matter how we look at it, the act of deceiving requires the intention to deceive. Thus it cannot be simply the consent of a deliberating will which first endows the action with an immoral quality—for that would require that it is the reflective will alone which constitutes the action as deceit.

A second difficulty with this view of moral volition is that it requires the moral intention always to be abstract. The deceiving of others cannot be viewed as intrinsically wrong but as wrong only because it conflicts with a higher and independent set of principles. The problem of moral judgment is thus represented in an unfortunately artificial manner. In judging a possible immoral action, we are to measure a line of action which has its own empirical motivation against a moral rule which might or might not be assigned to the action. The artificiality arises from the fact that the action we are tempted to perform is not the one that is judged. The action we judge is the original act as taken up within an altogether new context of volition. We do not ask whether deception is wrong but whether deception as consented to and adopted by a free and rational will is wrong. This makes it appear that actions are morally wrong only in the second or reflective intention. In an important sense Kant's ethics simply does not provide for intrinsically wrong moral actions and, in that regard, his moral theory is not rigorous enough. He has conceded far too much to the presumed innocence of the natural man.

Now it might be argued in defense of Kant that he regarded moral maxims (the rule implicit in an action) as actually constitutive of actions and, hence, as not second intentional. That is, I believe, the most satisfactory way in which to interpret his theory. The only difficulty with such an interpretation is that it requires the revision of some of Kant's most fundamental and most frequently reiterated doctrines. If we are to say that a moral maxim is constitutive of empirical motivation, we cannot regard the moral quality of an action as due simply to the consent that is given to it. Moreover, we must surrender the dichotomy between empirically contingent inclinations and moral volition. Again, the problem is the same as in the case of concepts. If we permit concepts to be intrinsic to sensible intuition so as to constitute an essential feature of the intentional act of sensing, we cannot hold that sensing and conceiving are completely independent operations. By the same token, if we grant that the moral will is active in shaping our inclinations, we cannot credit moral volition with a completely distinct sort of motivation. The same moral will would have to be operative at the empirical level in the *constitution* of action and at the reflective or transcendental level in the *judgment* of action. Instead of regarding moral judgment as the measuring of an intrinsically neutral action against an external moral standard, we would have to regard it as the will judging itself. In a way, of course, Kant wants to interpret moral judgment as the activity of the will in assessing its own volition. The assignment of a maxim to every concrete action is designed to provide for that possibility. Insofar as an action has a maxim (viewed now as a rule of volition) we can judge it morally by seeing whether or not it conforms to the requirements of the moral law. Although the general schema is sound, it simply does not go far enough. Because the maxim is external to the action, the moral agent can never decide whether lying is intrinsically wrong. He can only determine whether the adoption of the formal maxim which we hypothetically assign to lying might be morally wrong. Some of Kant's critics have charged that any action can be made to appear morally acceptable by assigning the right maxim to it. There is, I think, no way in which Kant can avoid this difficulty without revising his conception of motivation. Unless the moral intention can be shown to be that which is constitutive of the concrete act of lying, we can never be certain that we have appraised it correctly. A different moral rule (maxim) might make the act morally correct. Kant had a good bit of trouble in deciding what to say about the acceptability of lying on moral grounds. Part at least of his difficulty stems from the fact that for him a moral maxim is not identical with animating intention of the act to be judged.

The obverse side of this problem is that of determining when the moral law has been correctly applied. If the externality of the maxim allows for the possibility of alternative ways of construing one and the same material action, we can never be certain that we have applied the law correctly in attempting to implement it. If, in other words, the order of nature is independent of the order of moral volition, there is more than one way in which the former can be subsumed under the latter. We can simply choose our maxims in such a way that they are in formal accord with the requirements of the moral law and then attach them to our actions. As Hegel pointed out, depending on the meaning we assign to property, we can either abolish it or make it sacrosanct. This was clearly not the way in which Kant intended the moral law to work. Those critics who have accused him of appealing only to logical consistency have seriously distorted his conception of the moral law. At the same time, however, their criticism points to a genuine weakness in his theory. Even if we construe moral volition as a teleologically coherent unity of the will and grant that it must include material as well as formal conditions, we still have the problem of relating empirical motivation to rational volition. So long as this connection remains contingent, some degree of arbitrariness in the correlation of the two components cannot be avoided. That is the valid core of the objection to his formalism. If the moral law is to have teeth in it for the dishonest storekeeper, he must not be able to put a face on his action that will make it morally acceptable. More generally, no one should be able to alter the moral character of a contemplated line of action through his choice of a maxim.

A second move might be made to defend Kant's position by suggesting that he simply drew the line between inclination and moral volition at the wrong point. It might be argued that he chose too complex and too well developed a situation to illustrate the operation of moral judgment. He might well have selected a case where the empirical motivation is more conspicuously devoid of moral features. Kant did cite more elementary examples to illustrate his thesis and it is only fair that they be considered. The question whether human beings are naturally egoistic or altruistic had been widely discussed in the eighteenth century. Some moral philosophers based their reasoning on the assumption that men are naturally benevolent and others on the contrary assumption that they are naturally exploitive of others. Kant regarded the whole controversy as irrelevant since, in the first place, the issue raises an empirical rather than a philosophical issue and could not possibly be decided by a reflective analysis; secondly, he believed that, however the issues were to be settled, it would have no direct implications for ethical theory. Normative ethics must be based upon reason rather than nature. In his personal assessment of the empirical question Kant took a mediate position between the two extremes. He was convinced from his own observations that some men are naturally benevolent and sociable, and others self-seeking and aloof. Since these qualities are presumably the result of one's natural endowment, they would appear to be independent of moral volition and, thus, on a different footing from the storekeeper's dishonest project.

There is no doubt that the closer we come to man's original nature, the more plausible Kant's theory of inclination becomes. From even the most casual observation we can distinguish a variety of temperamental differences among our fellow human beings. Must we not analyze such characteristics as empirical, contingent, and devoid of volitional content? And, if so, must we not distinguish sharply between those dispositions which derive from our empirical nature and those which originate in the will? A distinction between empirically contingent motivation and reflective volition must surely be allowed. The only question is how the distinction is to be made and, especially, whether it must take the form of a duality between empirical and rational components of man's nature.

In refining the problem we should remind ourselves that the question must be assessed from the perspective of the agent rather than that of an observer. Kant appealed not to an instinct theory to account for the material process of human behavior but to purposive dispositions. As was noted earlier, even the most elementary action is conscious and makes use of a representation of its object. If we analyze it within the context of practical reason, therefore, a natural disposition to sociability must be at least dimly aware of its object. Thus, if a man is by nature sociable it cannot be by virtue of instinct. He must be aware of the fact that he both seeks and takes delight in the company of other persons. He need not, of course, be reflective and deliberate in his sociability. It may be natural and relatively spontaneous in the sense that he enjoys it without taking thought. But this does not mean that it is thoughtless. If thought is construed as a conscious intention and the understanding that is intrinsic to it, then human sociability cannot be thoughtless even when it is unreflective.

Sociability must be analyzed as a way of being related to other persons which entails the recognition of others and the understanding of the relatedness. The inclinations that are involved in sociability must represent others as the focus for the motivation. This much is given by the conditions which Kant specifies for the analysis of empirical processes. The problem before us is just how the intentions which are constitutive of sociability are to be linked up with moral volitions which may recast and redirect them. Does the intentionality of moral volition develop in complete independence of the natural themes of sociability or by the modification and development of those implicit themes themselves? We know that as social patterns of behavior are developed in the life of a person they assume complex intentional forms. The individual must choose eventually how he is to be related sexually to others as, also, what other persons are to mean to him within the various contexts of organized society. If it is granted that the forms of adult sociability are even more varied than in the case of children, and further, that such patterns appear to be indefinitely modifiable, can we avoid the conclusion that the original themes intrinsic to sociability are plastic and capable of being developed in a variety of ways? This conclusion might be avoided if we were to adopt a more naturalistic theory than Kant's and eliminate from our original dispositions the notion of a "representation." So long, however, as we regard conscious themes as constitutive of inclinations, we cannot look upon an inclination as developing independently of the theme itself. This entails that there is or can be no purely natural development of such dispositions as human sociability. We cannot infer from a given state of an individual in which his social disposition is assessed that it will develop in a uniquely determined direction. The reason is that freedom encompasses not only the rational will but the life of impulse as well.

If we are to preserve the unity of the self, there must be a continuity of some sort between developed forms of sociability in the adult and those inclinations which provide the original incentives for it. Sociability may take an exploitive or sadistic turn. In that event the individual treats others as the means for the gratification of his own ends. As in the case of the deception of others, such a sadistic disposition exhibits an intrinsic moral quality. Not, however, by virtue of the fact that a transcending will has imposed its objectives on natural tendencies. The intellect and the will must have played an internal role in the transformation of sociability into sadism. The moral will of a person does not develop independently of his empirical motivations, but in and through the latter as that power which gives them their more ultimate intentions. The moral will does not have to be brought into our natural inclinations from the outside, as it were; it is located at the very center of them from the outset. It is for this reason that when an explicit moral problem occurs it is already a question of the will judging itself. Because, in the material action, the will has projected a morally significant end for itself, this end can be judged reflectively by reference to the concept of a rational and responsible will. It is only because the will recognizes that it has played a role in the positing of the material end that it can judge the intention morally. And when it pronounces judgment it is not simply on the form of the action but the material context as well.

If we regard sadism as a conscious project of inflicting suffering on other persons for one's own enjoyment, we must regard it as intrinsically immoral. We would have things completely backwards if we were to interpret the moral evil involved in sadistic action as deriving solely from a violation of the moral law. Sadism is morally wrong for the simple reason that it wills the injury of other persons. Although it may be viewed reflectively as violating the ultimate canons of morality, it must be recognized as immediately and intrinsically wrong. We can, in fact, formulate the moral law only by specifying in general terms the quality of such a wrong action. We do not proceed to deduce materially wrong actions from an abstract principle but derive the abstract principle from reflecting on materially wrong actions. This does not entail, however, that we can only generalize wrong actions to provide a rule which covers them. We may find in the specific action the general moral intention which overreaches the action and, by implication, commits the individual to a world in which the action would be located. This is, I believe, the way in which Kant conceived of the operation of the moral law. The difficulty is that his anthropology does not provide adequately for the instrumentality of the moral will in everyday behavior. The dualistic overtones of his theory require us to regard the connection between them as tenuous rather than integral. It implies that empirical motivation is devoid of moral intentions and, further, that moral volition develops abstractly and thus, in independence of material concerns. If the problems entailed by Kant's formalism are to be avoided, the moral will must be regarded as continuous rather than discontinuous with inclination and natural desire. We would then have no acute problem of applying it to concrete situations since it would have been already at work in the constitution of them. Where the moral will has not been operative no moral problem can arise.

The point I wish to make is that it is impossible for a sociable disposition to be developed without maxims which serve to provide it with intentional meaning. I see no way of avoiding this conclusion unless we are willing to regard sociability as an instinctive mode of behavior. Since Kant was unwilling to regard it in that way, he is committed in principle to the thesis that maxims are constitutive of our social relatedness. The only question that arises is whether such maxims are to be construed as moral maxims. Kant did not want to regard them as moral since he wished to reserve moral maxims for reflective volition. But his theory proves to be inadequate for the *descriptive* analysis of those situations in which moral problems arise. Because his anthropology does not recognize pre-reflective moral intentions, he must attribute the moral intention exclusively to the will which assigns a maxim to the action as previously constituted. A moral act must thus be viewed as an empirically constituted act *plus* that rational motive of the will which is added to it through reflection. Some actions cannot be taken up into the context of the rational will and, hence, must be rejected. Not, however, because the intentional themes which constitute the action are immoral, but rather because the moral maxim assigned to them cannot fit into the legislation of pure practical reason. There is obviously an ambiguity here in the concept of action—and that is part of the problem. Action can mean an empirically motivated line of conduct which involves no deliberate volition, or it can refer to morally motivated action which is free and rational. Kant restricts moral action to the latter type of motivation. Thus we have two kinds of action going on at the same time whenever moral maxims are brought into play. There is, first, the empirically motivated act which is free of intrinsic moral intentions; and, second, there is the will to implement the maxim assigned to the empirical action. Moral volition includes empirical motivation only in that it takes up those empirical acts to which the moral maxim relates. But, even so, the moral volition does not will the material end as such. In even the most complex moral action, therefore, the empirical themes and the moral themes remain distinguishable.

In formulating his ethical theory Kant was anxious not to hold men responsible for the contingent facts of their empirical nature. He distinguished sharply between empirical dispositions and the moral use that is made of them. The natively reclusive man is morally innocent so long as he does not neglect his obligations to other persons. He can never be morally required to like other people or even to find enjoyment in their company. But he can bring himself to respect them and make all of his actions toward others conform to the conditions which follow from that respect. The reclusive man can do what he is morally required to do, namely refuse to give in to his negative feelings toward his fellow men. If that is a difficult task and a rigorous demand, it is far less exacting than the requirement to reorient one's natural feelings toward one's fellow human beings. Kant believed that it would be unreasonable to expect a man to change his feelings and emotions, since they are beyond his volitional control. And it would, indeed, be unreasonable if our feelings and emotions developed independently of our volition. If, however, the moral will plays a role in the constitution of our emotional life, there is no reason why we cannot modify it from within.

If Kant's anthropology entails that a man cannot be held morally responsible for those natural tendencies which run counter to the demands of morality, neither does it allow him to be given moral credit for a natural disposition that supports morally good ends. This doctrine has the unfortunate consequence that moral virtue must always appear to be reflective and deliberate. Where a natural disposition and moral volition share a common end, it is either a happy accident or the result of constraint on the part of the will. This has seemed to many of Kant's critics as a reversal of the proper order of evaluation, for it would appear that the man who assists his neighbor because his neighbor is in need is morally superior to the man who must do so by reasoning about it. The reflective goodness of the latter action would appear to be inferior to the unreflective altruism of the former. Kant allows, of course, for the development of morally conditioned dispositions. But this does not quite meet the objection, since the form of the volition is still external to the empirical motivation. It does not permit virtue to encompass both the empirical motivation and the reflective volition.

We must, of course, recognize the difference between a relatively immediate disposition to consider the interests of others and the acceptance of an explicit principle which requires it. The reflective will must not be confused with the pre-reflective and immediate volition of the individual. The question is not, therefore, whether reflective volition is identical with our pre-reflective attitudes and dispositions but whether the two are in any way continuous. Must we not bring both inclination and moral volition under the category of freedom? And must not both of them be regarded as motivations on one and the same self? How are we to preserve the unity of the moral agent unless we credit both the immediate action and the reflective volition as falling within the province of his responsibility? Rather than distinguishing between natural virtues as happy but contingent endowments and moral virtue as the product of reflective volition, it would seem preferable to make use of a single concept of virtue to embrace the two qualities. We could then regard moral intentions as both constitutive of empirical actions and as reflectively regulative of them. Moreover, by distinguishing between the reflective and pre-reflective expression of a unitary intention, we could avoid an artificial connection between the animating purpose of an action and the moral maxim that is associated with it. Moral legislation would then supply not simply the rational form of our actions but the material principles as well.

Kant's basic error derived, I believe, from his conviction that he could base his ethics on the pure concept of duty and, hence, the concept of a pure rational will. As soon as he attempted to supply examples and to consider how the moral law can be applied, he was forced to consider the question of empirical motivation. Since he did not develop a systematic aesthetic of the moral consciousness, he had to operate with provisional assumptions about empirical motivation. Although he was committed in principle to consider all facets of behavior under categories of freedom, his theory of "natural affections" prevented him from integrating the intentionality of impulse with the rationally determined will. The rational will is supposed to regulate and, if necessary, coerce a part of the self which tanscends it. Whereas our inclinations follow contingent empirical laws which cannot be modified by reflection, the moral will can be determined by pure reason. The dichotomy is too sharp for his theory to be able to explain how moral intentions can regulate the empirical self or even be relevant to the material purposes of the latter. Kant greatly underestimated the importance of a philosophical account of man's empirical nature. The general principles of his ethics require a more inclusive descriptive account of human existence than he was prepared to offer.

There are several conclusions to be drawn from this brief consideration of Kant's ethical theory. It is apparent, in the first place, that a normative ethical theory must offer a descriptive account of man as a morally responsible being. There are only two alternatives so far as the relation of an ethical theory to man is concerned. Either it must refer to man as an actual being and defend the principles of duty as a fact of man's existence, or it must relate to a hypothetical being. Ethical rules can be prescriptive, in other words, only if they enunciate laws for human freedom. To be categorically binding they must be inescapable. Kant was, therefore, on solid ground in attempting to justify his ethical principles by the appeal to man as a free and autonomous being and, conversely, justifying his conception of freedom by appeal to the moral law. He had to prove that freedom is a fact and that the principles of morality are laws of human freedom. His ethics thus required a metaphysical account of human existence. Ethics does not, however, merely presuppose a metaphysical theory of existence; it is itself a metaphysical theory. Only from a practical or moral point of view can we examine our role as agents. The analysis of man as a moral being thus explicates those categories which structure the world of freedom. Freedom is not merely a possibility or an ideal which might or might not be operative in the empirical world. It is a fact about human existence without which we would be unable to understand either knowledge or morality. Practical reason enjoys primacy over theoretical reason because it can analyze the free activity that is involved in cognition. To understand inquiry we must bring it under the categories of freedom and view it as a legislative function of an autonomous subject.

The second conclusion to be drawn from the examination of Kant's ethics is that the self cannot be divided into two distinct components, the empirical and the rational. It is unsatisfactory to equate the moral will with rational volition for when that is done the moral will can only be contingently related to empirical processes. If any actions are to be regarded as intrinsically right or wrong, a moral intention must be involved in the constitution of them. Moreover, to analyze a moral problem we must understand how the will can judge its material intentions by reference to a formal standard. Thus the possibility both of formulating norms and of applying them to conduct requires that the will perform both a constitutive and a regulative function. Normative ethical theory thus requires a theory of empirical motivation which includes the autonomous will as a legislative power.

But so, too, does our conception of man require the integration of the empirical and the rational. We must be able to understand how one and the same self can express itself through empirical desire and the pure moral will. Thus metaphysics and ethics have a common interest. They represent different facets of a common concern rather than separate and distinct modes of inquiry. Both must be comprehended by a unified theory of existence.

So far as either ethics or philosophical anthropology is concerned, the fact to be analyzed is the world as viewed from the perspective of human freedom. More specifically, it is the fact of human existence itself. To specify ethical norms is to enunciate the laws which should govern human conduct. The ought involved here is a normative ought which may or may not be honored by human beings. But in another sense it is a descriptive ought in that it specifies those liabilities which actually impinge upon men. The ought of moral duty cannot be optional, else it does not express a duty at all. To assert a moral imperative must be, therefore, to explicate a necessary condition of human existence. The categorical imperative must be a genuine liability.

The difficulties in Kant's ethical theory are not the result of a confusion of descriptive with normative analysis—as Moore alleges—but stem from an incomplete descriptive analysis. Although he began with what he termed "common morality," Kant separated the pure from the empirical part of morality too sharply and thus neglected to analyze the constitutive role of practical reason in shaping the world of empirical fact. In morality as in science we must begin with an empirical order that is categorically structured. Through his action man legislates for his everyday world whether or not he sets for himself an explicit moral end. He operates as a free being even where he fails to make of his freedom a principle of his action. To avoid the consequences of the Kantian duality between empirical and rational volition we must reexamine our conception of man's empirical nature. A satisfactory theory of human existence must be able to explain how pure moral volitions can arise on the foundation of everyday experience. The intentionality of moral volition must be integrated with the intentionality of empirical motivation. They cannot be regarded as processes which take place side by side, nor can they be related only externally as higher to lower faculty. The task before us is thus clearly set. We must, on the one hand, preserve the unity of the existing subject. And, on the other hand, we must explain how man as a moral agent can act in his situation within the everyday world. Kant has provided us with the basic perspective and the essential outline for achieving this twofold objective.

CONCERNING ETERNAL PEACE
–ETHICS AND POLITICS

Gerhard Funke

Immanuel Kant's essay *Zum Ewigen Frieden (Concerning Eternal Peace)* was published in 1795, the year of the Peace of Basel between Prussia and France, between a monarchical government of the "ancien régime" and the Directorate of a revolutionary state. In its subtitle Kant called his essay "a philosophical sketch."[1] His concern was, first of all, to contribute toward the establishment, *hic et nunc,*[2] of a system of law compatible with personal freedom, although he had no illusions about the actual situation of his time. Simultaneously, however, the essay deals with mastering a task which, because of man's own nature, is set for mankind as a whole, and which devolves upon every individual in his historical situation by virtue of his dual nature, involving causal necessity and freedom.

To be sure, "heads of state who can never get enough of war,"[3] or "practical politicians" accustomed to looking down "with greatest self-complacency" upon the philosopher as a "mere pedant" (as such "statesmen wise in the ways of the world" cannot help doing) will not take seriously the philosophers with their "empty ideas" who "dream this sweet dream"[4] of eternal peace. How much less can they take seriously the many individuals (philosophers in a "worldly" rather than a purely "academic" sense) who also indulge in such dreams. In view of this widely held opinion concerning all philosophers who do not cling to traditional political "principles of [practical]* experience," Kant felt called upon to emphasize that his own "opinions, hazarded with hope for fortune's favor [regarding their truth] and publicly expressed," would at least constitute no danger for state or society, and could therefore be presumed to be permissible.

Above and beyond these considerations, Kant's theory of eternal peace forms an important part of his philosophy of history. Although Kant added no explicit *Critique of Historical Reason* to his other *Critiques* (of "Pure Reason," of "Practical Reason," and of "Judgment")[5] it remains, nevertheless, just as certain that his concern with man in history[6] aims at discovering the preconditions for a (not yet attained but, certainly, in principle deducible) general rationale of freedom as a peaceful world order for mankind. Consequently, within the bounds of this systematic approach the task presents itself of attaining a [theoretically] valid, repeatable transcendental deduction of the envisioned future world order of peace, which —as will be shown later—must be at the same time a legal order based on reason, binding together all nations on earth. This task would thus be carried out in analogy to the transcendental deduction of the concepts of pure understanding in the first *Critique,* or to the transcendental deduction of the principles of pure practical reason in the second.[7]

That history literally "represents" the realm of freedom, as Kant suggests in the *Idea for a Universal History from a Cosmopolitan Point of View* of 1784, becomes evident in the following hypothetical [teleological] argument based on a supposed "intention of nature": Nature intended that man "develop completely on his own everything which goes beyond the [mere] mechanical regulation of his animal being,"[8] i.e., that he "acquire it free from all instinct, by means of his own reason."[9] This process has taken place in time and is perceivable in history; and Kant now undertakes to investigate the actualization of freedom in history.

---

*All terms in square brackets are insertions intended to clarify Kant's meaning.

His concern is with a "practical concept of freedom," not with a "speculative" one, "the latter being left completely to the metaphysicians."[10] In 1783 (in his review of Schulz's "Versuch einer Anleitung zur Sittenlehre") and in 1784 (in *Idea for a Universal History from a Cosmopolitan Point of View*) Kant's primary [methodological] approach is plainly nonspeculative. In the "Review" he says: "Where the situation in which I am to act at this moment originally came from may remain fully indifferent to me; I ask only what I have to do now, and for this freedom is a necessary practical pre-condition and an idea according to which alone I can judge the commandments of reason to be valid."[11] Everyone, even the "most hard-boiled sceptic," would have to confess that "when an act comes about, all sophistic doubts based on [the supposition of] universal delusion in appearance must disappear."[12] Human action always incorporates knowledge of some degree. In the same way, if human action is to be more than a causally determined process, and duty more than naked force, "the most resolute fatalist" must "act in every moment as if he were free"; and this idea of freedom would "actually bring about the act conforming to it."[13]

In the *Idea for a Universal History from a Cosmopolitan Point of View* Kant presents the problem at two levels: He develops it, on the one hand, based on [theoretical] principles in conformity with his system. On the other hand, he expands the theme hypothetically also. That is, whatever "concept of freedom of the will one may form from a metaphysical point of view, its manifestations, [i.e.] human acts, are, like every other phenomenon of nature, determined by universal laws of nature."[14] Phenomena act only upon other phenomena; yet they appear to represent more than this.

If, thus, within the realm of phenomena the laws of nature prevail universally, the further question remains as to how these phenomena can simultaneously be the manifestations of freedom within historical reality. This fact, however, is often spoken of, and "history, occupied with narrating these manifestations, allows us to hope that, in viewing the play of freedom of the human will in the large, we may be able to discover an orderly process in it," i.e., in history.[15] As a scientific discipline history may thus "be able to recognize what, in reference to the individual subjects, strikes us as being complicated and irregular, but what, in respect to the whole species [of man], is recognizable as a steadily progressing, although slow, development of his innate natural disposition."[16] This innate disposition is one toward reason and freedom.

"History" (as *historia rerum gestarum*) preserves "history" (as the essence of *res gestae*). Kant demonstrated in the *Critique of Pure Reason*[17] the "possibility of causality through freedom in connection with the universal laws of natural causality," i.e., he demonstrated that it is not self-contradictory to consider these two kinds of causality as being mutually compatible.[18] However, neither the reality nor the possibility of freedom was demonstrated or proven in the *Critique;*[19] for freedom can never be elicited from experience but must be treated as "a transcendental idea whereby reason is led to think that it can begin the series of conditions in the [field of] appearance by means of the sensibly unconditioned."[20] But, Kant observes, "nature does at least not contradict causality through freedom."[21]

Kant follows through on this theme in the *Critique of Practical Reason.*[22] Although speculative reason cannot attain knowledge above and beyond mere "experiential knowledge," it is quite possible for us to assume the existence of freedom together with the "principles and limits of pure theoretical reason."[23] The principle and inner possibility of freedom can therefore be developed because, "as far as we can conceive of it, transcendental nature [is] nothing other than nature under the autonomy of pure practical reason."[24] This assumption obviously extends the theoretical basis. However, *the way in which* freedom may appear within nature, or whether or not it appears at all, if left open in both *Critiques*.

Now, if, with respect to history, the whole question of freedom is not to remain purely theoretical, then it is of primary importance to demonstrate the possibility of a "transition" from the mode of thinking according to principles of nature to the mode of thinking according to principles of freedom,[25] and this entails acknowledging the effects of freedom in the world of phenomena.

However, it is a fundamental principle for Kant that "a vast gulf exists between the realm of the concepts of nature—the sensible realm—and the realm of the concept of freedom—the supersensible realm"[26] —so that by the theoretical use of reason no "transition" between these two worlds is possible, although the intelligible world can influence the empirical, for freedom is bound "to realize within the sensible world the purpose dictated [by its own laws]."[27] But the question still remains: How is freedom to realize this purpose, or how is this purpose to actualize itself?

This question Kant answers in his works concerning the philosophy of history; for it is in events, as temporal occurrences, and thus in history (if it is to happen at all anywhere or in any way) that the entrance of freedom into nature manifests itself in the appearance of law. "Law" is comprehensible only as the representation of an otherwise problematic factor which, inasmuch as it "obeys a principle of reason, on the one hand, belongs to the sphere of freedom, but which, on the other hand, as statute law governing the behavior of empirical individuals in society, belongs to the sphere of phenomena and hence to nature."[28] "Law" thus points to the appearance of reason.

It follows from this that philosophy of history, theory of freedom, the actuality of law and the idea of eternal peace are all interconnected, and that a "transcendental foundation" for them all can now be constructed, even though Kant does not expressly present one.[29]

In the *Idea for a Universal History from a Cosmopolitan Point of View* a structural outline of the principles of historical development is given in the form of nine theses, i.e., in a logical nontemporal progression. The result is the following hypothesis: Although man is certainly a creature of nature, he is one gifted with reason, and one who "can develop [his reason] fully only within the species [as a whole], not in the individual state."[30] Seen in this perspective, man is a historical being; and he is even more so when he has to develop everything which transcends "the mechanical system of his animal existence" completely "from within himself"[31] by means of his own reason, and therefore this development is not a quasi-automatic process but an act of free self-realization—provoked though it may be by the antagonism of the different dispositions of the individual persons.[32] Although at first far from being peaceful, this antagonism in the manifestation of the various dispositions is in practical respects advantageous, for, as its most important consequence, it compels the gradual attainment of "a universal civil society administering the law."[33] If the hypothesis that nature intends the development of "all its potentialities" proves to be true, then nature must also intend that reason, its gift to man, develop; and history is made necessary by the fact that "the highest intention of nature is realized only in society, and only in that society which [combines] the greatest freedom, and therefore a thoroughgoing antagonism, of its members with the most exact determination and protection of the boundaries of this freedom so that it [this freedom] may exist [together] with the freedom of others."[34] This intention can be fulfilled only through the development of *all* of nature's potentialities—including reason.

Now, reason always brings forth "law" and actualizes "law." The pre-condition for this is that a society be found "in which freedom under formal laws is united to the greatest degree possible with the compelling power of government, i.e., that a completely just civil constitution [prevail]." So long as such a society does not exist but man possesses reason, that society represents "the highest purpose of nature for mankind." Empirically considered, man is certainly "carved out of such crooked wood"[35] that nothing truly straight can be formed of him. He is "an animal which, when living among others of his species, is in need of a master,"[36] for otherwise everyone would misuse his freedom. It is precisely this misuse, possible in conception and actual in experience, that makes "the establishment of a perfect civil constitution"[37] and, ultimately, of an international legal order even more necessary now when the original unsociableness of ancestral individuals has reappeared as the quasi-natural unsociableness among nations. In this situation man, as rational being, "needs" history—a fact which can also be deduced from his empirical nature.

But now an objection arises to beginning our investigation with such an "historical" point of view. The objection is this: "Because men in their various endeavors do not act merely in accordance with instinct nor, in the main, like rational citizens of the world according to an agreed-upon plan, no planned history appears possible for them."[38] In this situation the question is: Under what conditions is a planned history conceivable? What do Kant's investigations of freedom and law and, consequently, of peace in history reveal? If the conditions leading to a meaningful interpretation of history are not presupposed, then we are confronted with "a nature moving without purpose" and "the disconsolate sequence of accidents *(das trostlose Ungefähr)* takes the place of the guiding light of reason."[39] Only the advance of reason can lead to a diminishing influence of man's empirical nature.

"Law," in the form of public law, of international law, and, finally, of international civil law, is the manifestation of reason in the world of phenomena. Its historical reality takes the form of "progress." According to Kant, we need not merely hope "chiliastically" for such development,[40] we may deduce its realization at some future time—provided it is true that, following every reversal (which results from the hypertrophy of freedom that is manifest in the arbitrary acts of individuals), reason in the individual always returns to that self-discipline demanded of the individual by reason itself. And just as individuals combine in order to counter the excesses of individual freedom by conceiving a legal system, by instituting it in practice, and by maintaining it, so the national states will, in time, combine and transcend the particularism of nations by instituting and respecting a world constitution.

With this conception of world history—which, "so to speak, has a guiding principle a priori"[41]—Kant does not mean to interfere with or eliminate the empirical study of history. He merely wants to demonstrate that history as a whole remains a meaningless sequence of events if no organizing principles are assumed for it, and that such principles can be deduced only from man's natural disposition to freedom and reason. In practice, the guarantee for the development of this disposition is not encountered in society until law in its manifold forms has been introduced. Freedom and "eternal peace" are the consequences of the full development of culture together with the realization of a universal—i.e., an international—order which, ultimately, means a "system of all nations which are in danger of affecting one another to their [mutual] disadvantage."[42]

With respect to man, however, the final purpose of nature can, for Kant, be only what is called "culture," i.e., "the development of the capability of a rational being for all possible ends whatsoever ([and] thus in its freedom)."[43] The way to this goal entails the establishment of a truly universal system of law, and with it the achievement of "eternal peace."

In the course of this development it is the task of the state to make it possible for each of its members to become a free and independent person. This means that "every member of a state should be not merely a means only but also an end and, by contributing to the possibility of the whole, should through the idea of the whole determine his own position and function."[44]

Necessity and reason bring man to the realization that national law, international law, and international civil law are indispensable. Kant therefore speaks of the legal status of "a federation according to mutually agreed upon international law,"[45] of "a theory based upon that legal principle which determines what the relations among men and nations should be,"[46] and of "always acting so that a universal state of nations of this kind may be established."[47]

In Kant's essay, *Religion Within the Bounds of Mere Reason,* the demand is made more clearly that, "in accordance with moral laws," man ought to "establish a power and a realm"[48] which "attains victory over evil and assures eternal peace for the world under its reign."[49] But even the attainment of this goal depends upon the existence of a "universal and authoritative international law."[50] And this means that an "international law which is effective" can itself "exist only within a federal union of free states"—where by "federation of states" is meant the union of those powers or nations "which, without coercive laws, guarantee to one another that freedom upon which an eternal peace can be based."[51] But states themselves must already be internally structured and organized on the basis of universal civil rights.

As far as the historical perspective is concerned, the situation is as follows: By including reason and freedom in the historical process Kant assumes as a hypothesis that the order of nature intends "that power and coercive force precede law; for, without the former, men themselves could not even be brought to the point of uniting to form laws." Historically, however, this situation does not suffice, for "the order of reason intends that afterwards [i.e., after the reign of power and coercive force] law regulate freedom and give it form."[52]

When it has finally become universal, the regulation of freedom through law makes "eternal peace" possible. However, the "guarantee of eternal peace" is based on the following: That which "gives this guarantee" is no other and no less than "the great artist Nature *(natura daedala rerum),* from whose mechanical processes [teleological] purpose shines forth visibly." This happens when "through the conflict among men harmony arises even against their will."[53] Here is the hidden "ground of unity." Without its assumption only the "mechanism of nature" would remain.

In the "Preliminary Articles" of *Concerning Eternal Peace*[54] Kant lists "prohibitive laws *(leges prohibitivae),*"[55] the observation of which is indispensable for the existence of any peace whatsoever. In the "Definitive Articles" he sets forth, in the form of [affirmative] precepts, the pre-conditions for the actual establishment of peace.[56] He is here concerned with the republican civil constitution[57] including civil law, international law, and international civil law.[58] That is, he is here concerned with the "federation of nations" as the result of international law,[59] and with international civil law based on the "conditions of universal hospitality."[60]

In the concrete situation the existence of eternal peace depends upon whether or not men progress in the improvement of the conditions of legal government; i.e., it depends upon whether or not they are able to advance from national law to the wider, the more universal forms of law;[61] for the "peaceful relationship among men living together is not a state of nature *(status naturalis),*"[62] but must be specifically and consciously "brought about";[63] and this is possible only through reason and freedom. The external freedom, initially necessary, may be explained as "the right to obey no other external laws except those to which I have been able to give my consent."[64] That one can take advantage of this "right" presupposes that a legal structure exists which already represents a certain degree of the realization of reason.

In the first of the two "Supplements" to the "Articles of Peace" Kant deals with the following theme: Man's undeniable egoism may be overcome, in the future as it has been in the past, by the disposition of reason to its own further development which already has resulted in the establishment of national civil rights as well as in the stipulation of universally binding laws within a national framework. This same trend leads us to expect the subsequent development of international law and of international civil law in accordance with a certain developmental "mechanism."[65]

The second "Supplement" makes a sarcastic reference to the fact that it is neither to be expected nor desirable "that kings philosophize or philosophers become kings"[66] because in *every* person "the possession of power inevitably ruins the free judgment of reason."[67] However, in order that the general goal of eternal peace and its pre-condition not be forgotten it is necessary that the "maxims of philosophers concerning the pre-conditions of the possibility of public peace" be consulted by the parties concerned, i.e., "by the nations that are armed for war."[68]

In his investigations into this problem Kant is in general quite realistic. He notes:

> that at present "our rulers of the world" have no money left "for public educational institutions and, in general, for anything that pertains to the best in the world" because "everything is already committed in advance for future war";[69]
>
> that one "cannot avoid a certain indignation" when one considers what men "do and fail to do upon the world stage" and finds in their actions much that is "woven out of childish evilness and destructiveness, and one does not know in the end what concept one should

form of our species which is so conceited because of its advantages";[70]

that, with respect to mankind, it is forgotten again that it "was not the purpose of nature that man live well but that he advance so far as to prove himself worthy of life and well-being by his behavior";[71]

that it is only a challenge "which awakens all abilities of man"; that a challenge motivates him "to overcome his inclination to laziness and [that] driven by ambition, the desire for power, and greed [he seeks] to attain status among his fellowmen";[72]

that therefore, nature ought to be thanked "for the envious, competitive pride, for the insatiable desire for possession or power," for without them, and in the precise meaning of Mandeville's maxim: "private vices, public benefits," the "excellent natural dispositions" in human nature would "sleep eternally undeveloped";[73]

that accepting a "perfectly just civil constitution" requires accepting a "state of compulsion" also, for "only necessity impels" man, who is "otherwise so fond of unbounded freedom," to take this step;[74]

that, considering his animal tendencies and his as yet imperfectly developed reason, man needs, at times at least, a master who will break his arbitrary will and force him "to obey a general will under which *everyone* can be free";[75]

that, finally, "as long as states apply all their energy to vain and brutal aims of expansion, nothing positive can be expected of them" and that, accordingly, "a long inner development of every body politic is necessary for the education of its citizens."[76]

In view of all this, no rapid progress can be expected here, and it must constantly be taken into account that "no state is safe against the others, not even for an instant, as far as its independence or its possessions are concerned."[77] All possible steps must therefore be taken in order that "a universal state of world citizenship may be brought about at some future time as the womb within which all natural dispositions of mankind are to be developed."[78]

With this insight the question of the relationship between politics and morality is touched upon in a general way. Moreover, "Appendix I" of *Concerning Eternal Peace* deals superficially with the "Conflict between Morality and Politics in the Intention towards Eternal Peace," while "Appendix II" deals no less tentatively with the "Harmony of Politics and Morality According to the Transcendental Concept of Public Law."[79] Among the "conflicts" we find that in the eyes of the "practical politician" morality remains "mere theory";[80] that, in fact, "glossing over the illegal principles of state" counts as "national prudence";[81] that anyone, "once he has power in his hands," will not allow his subjects "to dictate laws to him";[82] that it is inferable "from the nature of Man" that he will "never want what is necessary to the attainment of that goal which leads to eternal peace";[83] and, finally, that revolutions, "where they are brought about by nature itself," only serve "to gloss over an even greater oppression" instead of being understood as the "call of nature" to bring about now at least "a legal constitution based on principles of freedom."[84]

There is agreement, on the other hand, between politics and morality to the effect that the maxims developed in order to advance the purpose of a state of law must be made public; for "a maxim which I am not allowed to make public without thereby simultaneously frustrating my own intention"—an intention that "must be hidden if it is to be successful and which I cannot publicly endorse"—represents the opposite of that which can become universal, and thus disqualifies itself from being accepted a priori as an ethical principle. Whether political activity is carried out superficially or tentatively in agreement with the empirical nature of man, political reality will become meaningful only when it is in harmony with his intelligible character, i.e., with his rational character in a fully developed state.

Against the usual "political guiding principles": *fac et excusa* (i.e., to take advantage of the opportunity and to gloss over the act afterwards), *si fecisti, nega* (i.e., to deny the act later and to transfer the guilt to universal human nature), *divide et impera* (i.e., bring about conflict and evoke the appearance of helping the weaker);–against these so-called political maxims[85] the categorical imperative is to be brought into the conflict as the one subjective rule which can become universal and which can be stated briefly as follows: Act so that you can desire your maxim to become universal law. This imperative is only one, even though it may take various forms.[86] In its briefest form it demands: "Subject, act with objectivity."

From the obeying of such a rule there results ultimately nothing but the realization of the universal principle of freedom which establishes the employment of unlimited rationality within limited freedom in accordance with the framework of a system of universal civil law, of international law, and of international civil law within a society of moral beings.

We can summarize all this in Kant's own words: "Strive first toward the realm of pure practical reason and its righteousness, and your goal (the enjoyment of eternal peace) will come about of itself."[87] This statement is based on the conviction that a proper union of all individual wills, "when carried out consistently, can be at the same time, [and] even within the mechanism of nature, the cause which brings about the intended effect and makes the concept of law effective."[88] But, for Kant, the law is the focal point at every stage of human development: "Man's law must be kept holy, however much this may cost the ruling powers. Here one can divide nothing nor develop the hybrid of a system of law contingent on pragmatic considerations (of right and usefulness); rather, all politics must bend its knee before the former but may then hope to advance, although slowly, from level to level to where it will shine with a constant glow."[89]

"Eternal peace" thus becomes a moral task which, though entailed by the "principle of the moral politician,"[90] has yet to overcome all obstacles but which, because of a certain force of nature that is perceptible in the historical process, is inescapable for every individual. Thus, too, for Kant "eternal peace" is "not a vacuous idea but a task which, when resolved step by step, nears its goal steadily (because it is to be hoped that the periods of time in which progress is being made will become shorter and shorter).["9] [1] And "it is our duty constantly to work toward this end."[9] [2]

The question no longer is "whether eternal peace is a reality or an absurdity, and whether or not we deceive ourselves in our theoretical judgment when we assume the former; we [simply] must act *as if* this thing [eternal peace] did exist, even though perhaps it does not [actually exist], and must work toward its establishment and toward that constitution which, to us, seems best fitted for it . . . in order to bring it about and to put an end to the terrible war-making. Toward this goal [i.e., toward the establishment of peace] all states have up to now directed their internal institutions [only]."[9] [3] We must now aim at universal peace.

"History" thus becomes for each individual and for mankind as a whole the realization of practical reason. The antagonism between politics and ethics, i.e., the contradiction between the empirical and the intelligible character of man, will not be overcome until there really is a "transition" in man's "way of thinking"—a transition from the way of thinking in accordance with principles of nature to the way of thinking according to principles of freedom, which remains in all cases the task of the rational being.

Here we can learn from the "philosopher of Königsberg" what our duty is.

NOTES

1. All translations are the author's own, based on the *Akademie-Aus-gabe.* In this case Vol. 8, 341-86.
2. AA 8, 385.
3. AA 8, 343.
4. AA 8, 343.
5. Cf. Georg Picht, "Kants transcendentale Grundlegung des Völker-rechts," *Aufrisse,* Almanach des Ernst Klett Verlages, 1946-1971, Stuttgart, 1971, pp. 23-279; here p. 227.
6. Picht, p. 228.
7. *Kritik der reinen Vernunft,* A84 (AA 4, 68) B116 (AA 3, 99). *Kritik der praktischen Vernunft,* AA 5, 42.
8. AA 8, 17 and 19.
9. AA 8, 19.
10. Rezension von Schulz's *Versuch einer Anleitung zur Sittenlehre,* AA 8, 13.
11. AA 8, 13.
12. AA 8, 13.
13. AA 8, 13.
14. AA 8, 17.
15. AA 8, 17.
16. AA 8, 17.
17. B566. AA 3, 366.
18. Cf. "Erläuterung" B570, AA 3, 368.
19. B586, AA 3, 377.
20. AA 3, 377.
21. AA 3, 377.
22. Deduction of the Basic Principles of Pure Practical Reason. AA 5, 42.
23. AA 5, 43.

24. AA 5, 43.
25. Picht, p. 230; cf. the reference to the *Critique of Judgment,* AA 5, 176.
26. AA 5, 175f.
27. AA 5, 176.
28. Picht, p. 231.
29. Cf. Picht, pp. 227ff.
30. AA 8, 18.
31. AA 8, 19.
32. AA 8, 20.
33. AA 8, 22.
34. AA 8, 22.
35. AA 8, 23.
36. AA 8, 23.
37. AA 8, 24.
38. AA 8, 17.
39. AA 8, 18.
40. AA 8, 27.
41. AA 8, 30.
42. AA 5, 432.
43. AA 5, 431.
44. AA 5, 375.
45. "Ueber den Gemeinspruch: Das mag in the Theorie richtig sein, taugt aber nicht für die Praxis" (1793), AA 8, 311.
46. AA 8, 313.
47. AA 8, 313.
48. AA 6, 124.
49. AA 6, 124.
50. AA 6, 123.
51. Rudolf Reicke, *Lose Blätter aus Kants Nachlass* (Königsberg, 1898), p. 639.
52. *Lose Blätter,* p. 640.
53. AA 8, 361.
54. AA 8, 343-46.
55. AA 8, 347.
56. AA 8, 348-60.
57. AA 8, 349.
58. AA 8, 349.
59. AA 8, 354.
60. AA 8, 357.
61. AA 8, 349.
62. AA 8, 348.

63. AA 8, 349.
64. AA 8, 350.
65. AA 8, 356.
66. AA 8, 369.
67. AA 8, 369.
68. AA 8, 368.
69. "Idee zu einer allgemeinen Geschichte in Weltbürgerlicher Abschit," AA 8, 28.
70. AA 8, 17-18.
71. AA 8, 20.
72. AA 8, 21.
73. AA 8, 21.
74. AA 8, 22.
75. AA 8, 23.
76. AA 8, 26.
77. AA 8, 312.
78. AA 8, 28.
79. AA 8, 370 and 381, respectively.
80. AA 8, 371.
81. AA 8, 373.
82. AA 8, 371.
83. AA 8, 371.
84. AA 8, 373.
85. AA 8, 374-75.
86. Cf. the formulae in the *Fundamentals of the Metaphysics of Morals* (1785): "Act only according to that maxim by which you can will at the same time that it become universal law" (AA 4, 421). "Act as if through your will the maxim of your action were to become a universal law of nature" (AA 4, 421). "One must be able to will that a maxim of our acts become universal law: This is the absolute canon of the moral evaluation of them [i.e., of the acts] " (AA 4, 424). I should in my actions never act otherwise than so "that I could also will that my maxims become universal law" (AA 4, 402).
87. Cf. Karl Vorländer, *Kant und der Gedanke des Völkerbundes* (Leipzig, 1919), p. 50.
88. AA 8, 378.
89. AA 8, 380.
90. AA 8, 377.
91. AA 8, 386.
92. *Metaphysik der Sitten. Metaphysische Anfangsgründe der Rechtslehre* (1971). AA 6, 350.
93. AA 6, 354.

KANT'S PHILOSOPHY AND MODERN PHYSICS

W. H. Werkmeister

When, in 1924, Erich Adickes published his monumental two-volume work, *Kant als Naturforscher,* the relation of Kant's philosophy to modern science appeared to have been dealt with definitively. Two events, however, changed the picture radically. One was the development of modern physics itself, which, as quantum physics and wave mechanics, gave us a new conception of physical nature. The other was the critical examination of Adickes's work, which revealed that, because of his own essentially nonmetaphysical orientation, Adickes had done less than justice to Kant's conception of "metaphysical foundations of natural science."[1] Taking both of these facts into account I shall attempt here a re-evaluation of Kant's philosophy in relation to contemporary physics.

1

To begin with, it is important to note that Kant himself regarded the "critique of pure reason" as "a propaedeutic"—a "Vorübung" or preparatory exercise; whereas the knowledge "arising from pure reason alone" he called metaphysics. The latter is either speculative or practical. That is, it is "either *metaphysics of nature* or *metaphysics of morals.*"[2] We are here concerned only with the former. But what does Kant mean by *nature*?

In the *Critique of Pure Reason* we are told that "we have two expressions, *world* and *nature*"; that "the former signifies the mathematical sum of all appearances," whereas the term "nature" designates the same world of appearances "viewed as a dynamic whole,"[3] i.e., as in "thoroughgoing interconnection" in accordance with the principle of causality.

Sense impressions disclose to us a great variety of shapes and forms "out there"; but we cannot rest with this "mere rhapsody" of the givens. It is only by bringing the great diversity of impressions into the "unity of a system" that "ordinary knowledge" rises to "the rank of science": and only as "system" does knowledge satisfy "the essential ends of reason."[4]

The unity of the system is grounded in the idea which "determines a priori not only the scope of the manifold content [of the system] but also the positions which the parts [of that content] occupy relative to one another." And "no one [Kant maintains] attempts to establish a science unless he has an idea upon which to base it."[5]

However, Kant was sufficiently realistic to note that it is often only after a long period of collecting materials that it "becomes possible for us to discern the idea" which will integrate the aggregate of data into a system, and thus "to devise a whole architectonically in accordance with the ends of reason."[6] This goal can be achieved when we take the transcendental concept of reason to be "the concept of the totality of all the conditions for any given conditioned," which, as "the concept of the unconditioned," contains "the ground for the synthesis of the conditioned,"[7] and which, as pure concept of reason, "sets us the task of extending the unity of the understanding, wherever possible, up to the unconditioned."[8] The ultimate aim, in modern terminology, is the ideal of a "unified field theory."

As Kant sees it, "the most splendid example of the successful extension of pure reason" beyond the realm of the empirically given is mathematics,[9] which obtains "all its knowledge" through the "construction of concepts" (aided by a priori intuitions of space and time)[10] and proceeding by means of "axioms and demonstrations."[11]

But what is possible in mathematics is not possible in philosophy; for philosophical definitions "merely *explain*" concepts; they do not "*make*" them.[12] And since philosophy is simply what reason knows by means of concepts, it can have no axioms.[13] Still, the phenomena with which science is concerned are all appearances in space and time. To this extent they are all "extensive magnitudes";[14] and it is this fact which "makes pure mathematics, in its complete precision, applicable to objects of experience."[15] Here, then, we encounter the cognitive basis of all natural science insofar as that science consists of mathematically statable laws.

The classical example of such a science is, of course, Newtonian mechanics, to which, at the beginning of his career, Kant stood firmly committed. His *Universal Natural History and Theory of the Heavens* sets forth his attempt "to derive the formation of the heavenly bodies, as well as the origin of their movements, from the first [i.e., from the most primitive] state of nature by mechanical laws."[16] Kant was here concerned not only with the origin and development of the solar system, or of the galaxy of which it is a part, but also with all the galaxies which in their interactions constitute the universe. "Give me matter," he exclaimed, "and I will build a world out of it!" That is, he adds, "I will show you how a world shall arise out of it."[17]

The universe with which Kant is here concerned is the purely physical world. Are we in a position, he asks, to say: "Give me matter, and I will show you how a caterpiller can be produced?" And he answers with an emphatic No! "It should not be regarded as strange [he adds] if I dare to say that the formation of all heavenly bodies, the cause of their movements and, in short, the origin of the whole present structure of the universe will become intelligible before the production, by mechanical causes, of a single plant or a caterpiller is clearly and completely understood."[1][8]

2

Although Kant thus accepted as objectively valid the whole of Newtonian mechanics, he nevertheless wondered about the epistemological basis of that validity;[19] and this problem became the theme of the part of the *Critique of Pure Reason* that he called "Transcendental Analytic."

To be sure, in the "Transcendental Deduction" of the categories Kant had argued that, as experienced by us, nature is "the conformity to law of all appearances in space and time"; that this nature is "dependent upon the categories as the original ground of its necessary conformity to law," for only by means of the categories can we think objects; but that, in order "to obtain any knowledge whatsoever of [nature's] special laws, we must resort to experience."[20] This is so because the categories pertain "solely to the form of experience in general"[21] and "have no other possible employment than the empirical."[22]

Although the particular laws of nature can be determined only empirically, the broad principles basic to a "pure science of nature" (such as Newtonian mechanics) cannot be so derived but are indispensable presuppositions of the science itself.[23] They are "synthetic principles a priori" or "axioms."[24] To be sure, insofar as "philosophy is simply what reason knows by means of concepts, no principle deserving the name of an axiom is to be found in it."[25] But in the "Analogies of Experience" Kant provides an axiomatized basis for an interpretation of nature for which Newtonian mechanics served as a model but was not necessarily a complete equivalent.

To understand fully what is involved here, we must keep in mind that, as far as Kant is concerned, experience is not simply a matter of sense impressions. It consists rather of "sense impressions and judgments."[26] It is a "synthesis of perceptions"[27] which is "mediately subordinate to the legislation of reason."[28] Experience in this sense is the same as "knowledge by means of connected perceptions"[29] and, as such, is clearly "distinguished from mere . . . sensation."[30]

Since "nothing is really given us save perception and the empirical advance from this to other possible perceptions,"[31] "it follows that experience is possible only through a representation of necessary connections of the perceptions."[32] "Reason aims at systematic unity"[33] by viewing the given under its own integrative laws, so that, in the end, "there is only one single experience in which all perceptions are represented as in thoroughgoing and orderly connection."[34] As far as Kant is concerned, Newtonian mechanics was a first step toward that ultimate goal "to which reason seeks to approximate the unity that is empirically possible, without ever completely reaching it."[35]

In perfect harmony with this conception of the nature of experience Kant now formulates the "Principle of the Analogies": "Experience is possible only through the representation of a necessary connection of perceptions."[36] If it be argued that this "principle" follows analytically from Kant's conception of experience, it must be kept in mind that, as far as Kant is concerned, the "principle" and his conception of experience "rest on the synthetic unity of all appearances as regards their relation in time"[37] —which, in turn, is grounded in the synthetic unity of apperception.[38]

(1) Kant's "First Analogy" is the "Principle of Permanence of Substance." He states it this way: "In all change of appearances substance is permanent; its quantum in nature is neither increased nor diminished."[39] And he adds: "Everything which changes or can change belongs only to the way in which the substance . . . exists, and therefore to its determinations."[40]

To be sure, the traditional idea of substance is hardly acceptable in modern physics. In fact, as we shall see shortly, Kant himself modified it radically, bringing it much closer into alignment with contemporary interpretations. However, in every physical theory there is "a magnitude that remains conserved."[41] Kant's conservation principle thus has its counterpart in the "principle of the conservation of mass"[42] and the "principle of the conservation of energy"—two principles which were fused into one when, in the special theory of relativity, it was shown that for Lorentz-invariant frames of reference mass and energy are identical.[43] The principle of the conservation of mass-energy in this relativistic form is by no means analytically self-evident.[44] On the contrary, it is in the strictest Kantian sense a "synthetic principle a priori"; and one can predict that for every future Lorentz-invariant theory the conservation principle must be valid.[45]

(2) The "Second Analogy" or the "Principle of Causality" Kant states in this way: "All alterations take place in conformity with the law of the connection of cause and effect."[46] This principle is, in effect, a generalization of Newton's First Law of Motion: Any body at rest or in rectilinear uniform motion will remain at rest or in rectilinear uniform motion unless acted upon by an external force.[47]

Crucial to Kant's argument in defense of this principle is the fact that all changes take place in time. That something *may* happen is but an anticipation of a possible experience. The experience becomes actual when antecedent conditions determine its occurrence at a specific time in accordance with discernible laws.[48] That is to say, "the condition under which an event invariably and necessarily follows is to be found in what precedes the event"[49] and determines its occurrence in time. For this to happen, "the substances must stand, immediately or mediately, in dynamic community."[50] The specific laws which govern this dynamic relationship must be empirically discovered. The Second Analogy asserts merely the broad principle of causality.

Can this principle be maintained in the light of rather revolutionary developments in modern physics?

The basic problem is here the relation of the "principle of causality" to Heisenberg's "principle of uncertainty."[51] But it is essential that we understand that the latter merely asserts that in the microregions of physical reality we cannot determine at the same time the position and the velocity of an elementary particle with sufficient precision to make accurate predictions concerning the future position and/or velocity of that particle. This is so, Heisenberg explicitly states, because "the interaction between observer and object causes uncontrollable and large changes in the system being observed."[52] That is, in the microregions of subatomic particles the uncertainty in our knowledge is itself the result of our causal interference with the phenomena under observation.

To be sure, if we interpret the principle of causality as meaning that "whatsoever can be predicted with certainty is causally determined," then we must abandon it as far as sub-atomic phenomena are concerned; but in this sense the principle was never really "in force." When we take the principle of causality to mean what it normally means, namely, that "noth-ing happens without being determined by antecedent condi-tions," then quantum mechanics has in no way undermined its validity.[53] The fact that in certain situations we are unable, actually or even in principle, to discern the antecedent causal conditions of some particular phenomenon is no argument against the principle itself—least of all when we know that our failure is itself the result of a causal interference with the relevant conditions.

(3) Kant's "Third Analogy" is the "Principle of Coexist-ence": "All substances, as they can be perceived to coexist in space, are in thoroughgoing reciprocity."[54] It roughly corre-sponds to Newton's Third Law of Motion: "To every action there is always an equal and opposite reaction."

The three Analogies together, but especially the Third, "por-tray the unity of nature in the connection of all appearances under certain exponents which express nothing save the relation of time. ... [They] thus declare that all appearances lie, and must lie, in *one* nature."[55] To this Kant adds, in the third "Postulate of Empirical Thought," that "that which in its connection with the actual is determined in accordance with universal conditions of experience, exists necessarily."[56]

Since the totality of the conditions for any given conditioned is never given in experience but is a concept of pure reason, "extending the unity of the understanding, where possible, to the unconditioned" is at least a task for us—the task, namely, "of so directing the understanding that, while it is extended to the uttermost, it is also at the same time brought into complete consistency with itself."[57] In other words, it is "peculiarly distinctive of reason" that "it prescribes and seeks to achieve its systemization" by establishing "the connection of its parts in conformity with a single principle," that is, by projecting a unified system in which all knowledge obtained by the under-standing is "connected according to necessary laws."[58] It is not saying too much, I believe, when we assert that this Kantian theme is manifest throughout the history of science and but anticipates in the abstract contemporary efforts to establish a unified field theory in physics.

I shall return to this problem shortly.

3

Although Kant always regarded Newtonian mechanics as a model of scientific knowledge, it would be a mistake to think of him as adhering strictly and in every respect to Newton's ideas. We have seen already that his views are at least reconcilable with other interpretations of nature. We find more evidence of this fact in the "Antinomies" as developed in the *Critique of Pure Reason.*

In order to understand what is involved here we must keep in mind Kant's insight that theories are not simply derived from given data but are projections of reason for the interpretation of what is given in sense perception. And it is not really a surprise that "the facts" may be reconcilable with theories which differ in various respects. In the end, of course, such conflicts in the interpretation of given observational data may be eliminated either by conclusively disproving all but one of the conflicting theories, or by developing a new theory which transcends the conflict. The history of science provides many examples of this kind. In fact, the progress of science consists in part at least of just such achievements. Newtonian mechanics, for instance, is now seen as but a special case of relativity and quantum physics.

When we approach Kant's presentation of the "Antinomies of Pure Reason" from this angle, they take on a new significance.

We have seen already that, as far as Kant is concerned, "reason unifies the manifold concepts [of the understanding] by means of ideas."[59] These ideas, however, "never allow of any constitutive employment,"[60] although "everyone presupposes that this unity of reason accords with nature itself."[61] Actually, however, we deal here only with "the regulative capacity" of ideas, and with their function "in relation to the systematic employment of reason in respect of the things of the world."⁶ ² Or, as Kant also puts it, reason occupies itself solely with prescribing "to the understanding its direction towards a certain unity of which [the understanding] itself has no concept"⁶ ³ and thus of demanding "the absolute whole of all appearances"—which, nevertheless, "is only an idea."⁶ ⁴ What Kant gives us in the "Antinomies" is a demonstration that, with respect to certain facts of experience, mutually contradictory theories may be considered as equally valid, and that no empirical data or logical reasoning, or both together, are sufficient to decide between them.⁶ ⁵

To be sure, Kant himself argues that the antinomies should lead us to an investigation of "whether the object of controversy is not perhaps a deceptive appearance which each vainly strives to grasp."⁶ ⁶ But a solution may not be attainable because the ideas which give rise to the antinomies all pertain to "the absolute whole of all appearances," and this "can never be given *in concreto.*" "It remains a *problem* to which there is no solution."⁶ ⁷

Modern science finds this conception of alternative interpretations of reality quite congenial. Consider, for instance, Kant's "First Antinomy." Thesis: "The world has a beginning in time, and is also limited as regards space."—Antithesis: "The world has no beginning, and no limits in space."⁶ ⁸ What Kant here envisages is in all essentials the contrast between the so-called "big bang theory" and the "steady state theory" of modern scientific cosmology.⁶ ⁹

Or consider Kant's "Second Antinomy." Thesis: "Every composite substance in the world is made up of simple parts, and nothing anywhere exists save the simple or what is composed of the simple."—Antithesis: "No composite thing in the world is made up of simple parts, and there nowhere exists in the world anything simple."⁷ ⁰ Here again we have the modern counterparts in the corpuscular theories, on the one hand, and the field theories of matter, on the other.⁷ ¹

What all this comes down to is that "the unity of reason is in itself undetermined" as to the specific content of cognition, and that the idea of reason, as "an analogon of a schema of sensibility," provides "only a rule or principle for the systematic unity of all employment of the understanding."⁷ ² When such an idea is regarded as constitutive the conflicts revealed in the Antinomies are unresolvable contradictions. But when the ideas of pure reason are taken to be merely regulative principles, there is no real conflict. There are only those "differences in the interest of reason" which give rise to differing modes of thought whereby reason "endeavors to obtain satisfaction."[73]

So understood, the integrative interest of reason, though leading to conflicting cosmological theories, is in the end only a challenge to us to strive toward ever more comprehensive integrative systems—a fact clearly reflected in the history of modern science.

4

I have stated earlier that, from the very beginning, Kant accepted Newtonian mechanics as an objectively valid science of nature, and that in the "Analogies of Experience" he attempted to develop an axiomatic foundation for it. This does not mean, however, that Kant never went beyond Newton in essential respects. He in fact did so in the *Metaphysische Anfangsgründe der Naturwissenschaft* of 1786,[74] and in the projected "Uebergang" from the metaphysical foundations to physics proper in the *Opus postumum.*

Kant's basic theme is that "all natural science proper requires a pure part, upon which the apodictic certainty sought by reason in such science can be based."[75] That is, "natural science presupposes a metaphysics of nature."[76] And since the fundamental determination of any object of the external senses must be motion, natural science and its metaphysics must both be concerned with motion, be it pure or applied;[77] and the space in which the motion occurs must itself be an object of experience, i.e., it must be "empirical space."[78] This insistence upon space itself as an object of experience, i.e., as "empirical space," is crucial for Kant's arguments from here on out. But let us note also his explicit statement that "in every special doctrine of nature only so much science proper can be found as there is mathematics in it."[79]

In chapter 1 of the *Metaphysical Foundations* Kant effectively demonstrates the relativity of all rectilinear uniform motions. As he puts it: "Every motion as object of a possible experience can be viewed at will either as motion of a body in a space that is at rest, or as rest of the body and motion of the space in the opposite direction with equal velocity."[80]

Lest we draw an unwarranted conclusion from this statement, let me add at once that Kant is here propounding Galileo's and not Einstein's principle of relativity. What Kant's thesis amounts to is that we have no *mechanical* means of distinguishing between rectilinear uniform motion and rest. A set of simple transformation equations easily leads from one interpretation to the other. It is merely a matter of the reference system relative to which we consider a given body.

However, this classical principle of relativity turned out to be in contradiction with the results of the Michelson-Morley "ether-drift" experiments which revealed the constancy of the velocity of light irrespective of any reference system. It was this conflict of principle and fact that Einstein resolved by discarding the notion of absolute simultaneity, thus extending the principle of relativity beyond its classical form.[81]

So far, however, we have considered only rectilinear uniform motion. Newton, it will be remembered, had advanced three arguments in defense of absolute motion. The second of these was based upon the observable effects of "circular motion"; "for [he had said] there are no [centrifugal] forces in circular motion that is purely relative, but in a true and absolute circular motion, they are greater or less according to the quantity of motion."[82] Kant found this argument unconvincing, for it does not prove motion with respect to empty space.

To be sure, Kant admits that "circular motion can be given as *actual* motion in experience," for the centrifugal forces do produce observable effects; and so "it does indeed seem to be absolute motion."[83] But, Kant continues his argument, while circular motion per se does not change its location in space, "it exhibits a continuous dynamic change of the relation of matter within its space"—a change which is demonstrable as "a constant diminution of the attraction" between opposite particles of the rotating body. Thus, "one can represent the earth as rotating about its axis in infinite empty space and can prove this motion by experience," observing the effect of the centrifugal force. "But the change of the earth's relation to the starry heaven . . . is a mere appearance which can proceed from two actually opposed causes" and, therefore, is "only relative motion." It is, nevertheless, "true motion," for it reveals "the reciprocal continuous withdrawal of each part of the earth (outside of the earth's axis) from every other part that lies at an equal distance from the center of the circle in the line of this circle's diameter that runs through both of these parts."[84] To put it differently: circular motion, although true motion, is not absolute; for it can be empirically demonstrated only by way of the relation of one material particle to another, and not by way of a relation to empty space. "The motion of [the two particles of matter] is here not relative to the space surrounding them but only to the space between them . . .; and hence this motion is again only relative. Absolute motion would be only that motion which belongs to a body without a relation to any other matter."[85]

With this line of argument Kant had clearly abandoned Newton's position and had moved toward a conception of universal relativity which found its culmination in Einstein's general theory. What Einstein realized, and Kant did not, was that the laws of nature are invariant relative to all systems of reference *plus their respective gravitational fields.*[86] This conception of relativity is not a generalization based upon observational data, but is a principle of the understanding, synthetic in character and employed a priori as a rule for the interpretation of empirical data. Kant would have had no difficulty in accepting it as such.

5

The most far-reaching changes in our conception of physical reality have been brought about by modern quantum physics.

Newton stood firmly committed to an atomistic conception of matter. As he put it: "God, in the beginning, formed matter into solid, massy, hard, impenetrable, movable particles, of such sizes and figures, and with such other properties, and in such proportions of space, as most conduced to the end for which he formed them. These primitive particles, being solids, are incomparably harder than any porous bodies compounded of them; even so hard, as never to wear, or break in pieces."[87]

This conception of solid atoms as ultimate has been abandoned in contemporary physics.[88] We no longer need to speak of particles at all. "For many experiments it is more convenient to speak of matter waves";[89] and we know from relativity theory that matter can be transmuted into energy, and energy into matter. Not only have atoms been broken down into electrons, protons, and neutrons, but, beyond these, still other elementary particles—such as positive electrons and mesons—have been found; and there is evidence of the existence of still other elementary particles whose extremely short lifetime has so far made their actual discovery questionable. However, as far as we know, all elementary particles can be created from kinetic energy. This means the complete mutability of matter; and the ultimately real may perhaps best be regarded as energy, of which "material particles" are but different manifestations. Such an interpretation, I submit, is what Kant himself would have supported.

I shall argue my point in two ways: first negatively and then affirmatively. In support of my negative argument I refer briefly to some of Kant's explicit statements in the *Opus postumum.* There we read, for example, that the "corpuscular philosophy" is "a nest of fabrications." "The physico-dynamic [interpretation] is the correct one."[90] This is so because "no matter consists of simple parts,"[91] for "atoms do not exist; every part of a body is always again divisible into infinity," and "empty space is no object of possible experience."[92] It is therefore nonsensical to speak of "atoms and the void" as ultimate.

On the affirmative side of my argument I refer to Kant's *Metaphysical Foundations of Natural Science,* chapter 2. There Kant argues (a) that "matter is divisible into infinity";[93] (b) that it "fills space, not by its existence"[94] but by "the repulsive force of all its parts";[95] (c) that its "impenetrability" is therefore only "relative";[96] (d) that "the possibility of matter requires a force of attraction, as the second essential fundamental force," for if there were only its repulsive force, matter "would disperse itself to infinity"; strictly speaking, "there would then be no matter at all";[97] (e) that, if there were "mere attraction, without repulsion," matter would also not be possible;[98] (f) that neither of the two forces can be "separated from the other in the concept of matter."[99] And so Kant concludes: "All that is real in the objects of our external senses ... must be regarded as moving force. ... The so-called solid, or absolute impenetrability [of the Newtonian atoms], is banished from natural science as an empty concept."[100] Matter is "reduced to nothing but moving forces": "the repulsive forces in general and the attractive forces in general."[101] Or, as Kant puts it in the *Opus postumum*: "Through the moments of the moving forces matter must be made dynamically into an object of the senses."[102]

6

Kant, of course, was not familiar with Maxwell's interpretation of electromagnetic phenomena or with the much later Schroedinger wave-equations of matter. Both of these, in effect, treat space itself (aside from its being filled by matter) as the ground of the phenomena so described. But Kant also insisted that "space itself, conceived as object of possible experience, is the elementary matter."[103]

For Kant, however, there now arose a new problem; for he found it difficult to conceive forces as efficient causes of motion without some substance as their subject.[104] And so Kant argues that "basic to all actively moving forces of matter there is an originating *(uranfängliche)*, undiminished, infinitely continuous, and internally moving matter upon which the possibility of all bodies depends, which is deprived of all properties that can be moved only mechanically, ... and is effective dynamically only through continuously alternating attraction and repulsion."[105] Without this "universal basis of the moving forces," space itself "would be merely an idea and not a real whole of objects of possible perception."[106] In fact, the sole quality of this primordial "matter" is "that of being sensible space."[107]

Kant calls this space-equivalent "matter" variously "Wärmestoff" and "Aether." I shall simplify matters by referring to it consistently as Ether (with the capital E, in order to distinguish it from the ether of an older physics). So understood, Ether is, "as it were *(gleichsam)*, the hypostatized space itself in which everthing moves,"[108] and "whose motion originates all motions."[109] It is the ultimate objective ground of all physical phenomena[110] and "the basis of the possibility of *one* experience."[111] Or, as Kant also puts it: It is "nothing other than the universal basis of the moving forces of matter in experience, in so far as experience is *one*."[112] It is "the first mover *(primum mobile at mouens)*."[113] It must be postulated "because the moving forces of matter must begin with some sort *(irgend einer)* of motion."[114]

The conception of "a first mover appears to presuppose a will as efficient cause." Kant finds, however, that "the agitation of matter seems to maintain itself by itself perpetually *(ewig)*";[115] for, as he puts it, "a motion which starts by itself (i.e., has a beginning in time) must also continue to persist in the same measure"; and this, Kant finds, is possible only through a continuous alternation of attraction and repulsion within the Ether itself.[116] "One can conceive the Ether," we are told, "as primordially left to its own attraction. Out of this originates a concussion *(erschütternde Bewegung)* which constantly continues."[117] But it is counteracted by an equally primary repulsion. The interaction of these two forces sets up undulatory or vibratory motions.[118] Everything else depends upon them.[119]

How far removed from modern quantum physics is Kant's interpretation here? Consider for a moment Schroedinger's interpretation of the atom in terms of wave mechanics. The basic conception here is that the atom is a vibrating three-dimensional system consisting of a "fundamental" and its "overtones." The picture of electrons moving in a field of force has been replaced by that of an infinitely extended field of waves which generates local regions of maximum vibrations, the atomic nucleus being the "center" of such a region and therefore the "fundamental." The electrons around it are conceived as its "overtones."

Although this wave-theory of matter accounted for most atom-related phenomena, a number of difficulties remained. These, however, were also accounted for by Dirac's far-reaching revision of quantum and wave mechanics. Where we used to think that we could draw a picture or construct a model of what is actually going on in the microregions of physical reality, we must now admit that at best we can only create in our imagination a "vehicle for calculation" which enables us to derive from one basic "wave equation" all quantitative values otherwise obtained by experimental methods. Kant would certainly have approved of this development, for it confirms better than anything else could his contention that we comprehend not things-in-themselves but only what our minds have created, namely, the integrative interpretation of perceptual data in accordance with principles of reason.[120] Physics is no longer "empirical" in the old sense;[121] but Kant's epistemological considerations readily accommodate the modern developments. He would be especially pleased, I am sure, to find that his own interpretation of physical reality in terms of "vibrations" and "undulations" has found its modern counterpart in contemporary wave mechanics.

7

Physics, Kant maintains in the *Opus postumum,* is "the elementary system of the moving forces of matter insofar as these are the causes of perceptions."[122] But physics in this sense is simply a science of inorganic nature.[123] The primary forces, however, are "connected with the whole universe, because space and time are an absolute unity";[124] and "the whole universe" includes organisms as well as purely physical bodies. As Kant puts it: "Nature organizes matter in manifold ways not only according to kind but according to levels as well. . . . The organizing forces of our life-giving globe have organized even the plant and animal species in such a way that they (man not excepted) form together links in a chain: not only as to their nominal character (of similarity) but according to their real character (of causality), according to which they depend upon one another for their existence. This is a fact which points to a world-organization (for unknown purposes) even in the system of the stars."[125]

In the actual interpretation of organisms Kant starts from the initial thesis that "living matter does not exist, only a living body";[126] and that such a body is "possible only through purposes."[127] After all, "organic beings are those of which and in which every part exists for the sake of the other,"[128] as if the whole were but the manifestation of a purpose. This means that "organic bodies are natural machines" and must be interpreted as such.[129] But they are machines which are "effective because of their own [inner] force."[130] That is to say, "an organic body is a machine which creates itself as to form,[131] whose moving force is at the same time means and end."[132] But since a machine can be thought of only as an artifact *(Kunstprodukt)*, as "the work of an efficient cause endowed with understanding," we may interpret the living organism in this way also, although no such cause of it is actually found anywhere.[133]

The possibility of organic bodies cannot be understood a priori. The very concept of them must come from experience.[134] Kant is emphatic on this point. However, we do know ourselves as a living organism[135] and thus know at least one organic body empirically. But if we now interpret the organism as a machine, i.e., as "in its form a purposively constructed body," then it is impossible to maintain that its organization is entirely the result of the moving forces of matter. It is then necessary to assume some Being outside the organic body as "mover" which is efficient in accordance with purposes. "Whether this Being (perhaps a world-soul) possesses understanding or merely a capacity which, in its effects, is analogous to the understanding—the resolution of this problem lies beyond the limits of our insight."[136] But this "does not justify us in assuming that the efficient cause is a soul dwelling within the body" or is a world-soul outside the body. Kant thus rejects both, vitalism and supernaturalism, and maintains that all we can do is interpret the cause "in analogy to an intelligence," i.e., as a cause which we cannot render intelligible in any other way.[137] Although the idea of purpose is thus the guiding principle in our interpretation of living bodies, the constitutive processes of their formation are, nevertheless, subject to the laws of physics and chemistry only.[138] That is, the concept of purposiveness is merely a regulative idea which gives understandable and coherent meaning to the physical processes involved in body-formation and maintenance, without disrupting the overall scientific picture of the world we live in.

Thoroughly empirical in attitude and approach, this interpretation of living forms is in complete harmony with the best of our scientific tradition.[139] Here again Kant's views are in astonishing agreement with the insights of modern science. And with this I rest my case.

NOTES

1. See in particular Erich Adickes, *Kant als Naturforscher* (Berlin: Walter de Gruyter; Vol. 1, 1924; Vol. 2, 1925) 1: 145-232 and 353-370.
2. A841/B869.
3. A418/B446, and the footnote added in B (B446).
4. A832/B860. See also A644-5/B672-3.
5. A834/B862.
6. A835/B863.
7. A322/B379.
8. A323/B380.
9. A712/B740.
10. A713/B741.
11. A726/B754.
12. A730/B758.
13. A732/B760.
14. A162/B203.
15. A165/B206; A170/B212.
16. Akademie-Ausgabe von *Kants Gesammelten Schriften*, 1, 221, 5-9.
17. AA 1, 230, 1-3; 247-306. La Place's *Exposition du Système du Monde* was not published until 1796, or 41 years after Kant's work.
18. AA 1, 230, 16-26.

19. *Prolegomena to Any Future Metaphysics,* Carus translation as revised by Lewis White Beck (Indianapolis: Bobbs-Merrill, Library of Living Arts, 1950), p. 43: "There is then in fact a pure science of nature, and the question arises, *How is it possible?* " AA 4, 295.

20. B165. Cf. B263: "Empirical laws can exist and be discovered only through experience."

21. A125.

22. A146/B185. In particular, they yield no knowledge in the metaphysical speculations of pure reason alone.

23. B128. —The failure of "the illustrious Locke" and of David Hume to recognize this fact invalidates their positions. Locke "opened a wide door to *Schwärmerei* (reverie)," and Hume "gave himself over entirely to *scepticism.*" Kant proposes "to make trial whether it be not possible to find for human reason safe conduct between these two rocks."

24. B17f: "Natural science (physics) contains synthetic judgments a priori as principles. I need cite only two such judgments: that in all changes of the material world the quantity of matter remains unchanged; and that in all communication of motion, action and reaction must always be equal."—See also Paul Drossbach, *Kant und die Gegenwärtige Naturwissenschaft* (Berlin: Dr. Georg Lüttke Verlag, 1943), pp. 40f.

25. A732/B760.

26. *Prol.,* p. 51. AA 4, 304.

27. A764/B792.

28. *Prol.,* p. 113. AA 4, 364.

29. B161.

30. B218f.

31. A493/B521.

32. B219.

33. A568/B596.

34. A110.

35. A568/B596. —Gottfried Martin, referring to Kant's statement (B165) that "nature in general" is "the conformity to law of all appearances in space and time," argues that "such nature is completely determined through Newtonian laws," and is therefore "a purely mechanical system." See Gottfried Martin, *Immanuel Kant: Ontologie und Wissenschaftstheorie* (Berlin: Walter de Gruyter, 4th ed. enlarged, 1969), p. 78. Martin does not consider other possibilities.

36. B218, —A180/B222: "An analogy of experience is only a rule according to which a unity of experience may arise from perception.

... It is not a principle constitutive of the objects ... but [is] only regulative."

37. A177/B220.

38. A106. —A108: "This transcendental unity of apperception forms out of all possible appearances, which can stand alongside one another in one experience, a connection of all these representations according to laws." See also B137-40.

39. B224.

40. A183f/B227.

41. Carl Friedrich von Weizäcker, "Kant's 'First Analogy of Experience' and Conservation Principles in Physics," *Synthesis* special issue: *Kant and Modern Science* 23 (1) (1971): 75. See also Werner Kroebel, "Kant und die moderne Physik," *Studium Generale* 7 (1954): 531: The principle is simply "the presupposition of lawfulness in nature in general; for this ceases when process-determined parts disappear into nothingness or can be added out of nothing."

42. W. H. Werkmeister, *A Philosophy of Science* (Lincoln: University of Nebraska Press, Bison paperback, 1965), p. 285. The principle was first formulated by Lavoisier in 1775: "In every operation there is an equal quantity of matter before and after the operation; the quality and the quantity of the principle elements is the same, and there are only changes, only modifications."

43. See Albert Einstein, "Ist die Trägheit eines Körpers von seinem Energieinhalt abhängig? ," *Annalen der Physik* 18 (1905): 639-41.

44. Cf. von Weizäcker, "Kant's 'First Analogy' ...", p. 76: "Theoretical physicists have come to appreciate more and more the fact that the principle is not self-evident." And p. 93: "As long as we remain in the domain of existing physics [1971], we will find Kant's results sustained." Heisenberg, on the other hand, has argued that "no physicist would be willing to follow Kant, if the term 'a priori' is used in the absolute sense that was given it by Kant," Werner Heisenberg, *Physics and Philosophy: The Revolution in Modern Science* (New York: Harper & Brothers, 1958), p. 88. But Heisenberg is here obviously misreading Kant, as he does in other places also: pp. 90-91, 124, 127, etc., but especially p. 92: "It will never be possible by pure reason to arrive at some absolute truth." This impossibility is exactly what Kant means to demonstrate. See his letter to Christian Garve, dated August 7, 1783: "Do have the kindness to take another hasty view of the whole and note that it is not metaphysics at all with which I am concerned in the *Critique,* but a completely new and hitherto untried science, namely, *the*

critique of a reason which judges a priori." *Briefwechsel* (Hamburg: Felix Meiner, 1972), p. 228.

As to Heisenberg's contention that Kant's theory has been invalidated by modern physics, see Heinrich Kaestner, "Kant und die Moderne Naturwissenschaft," *Zeitschrift für Philosophische Forschung* 18 (1964): 119: "Es ist unbegreiflich, wie Heisenberg zu einem derartigen Fehlurteil kommen konnte."

45. Ibid., p. 77.

46. B232.

47. Robert Boyle (1627-91) had already prepared the way for such a generalization with statements such as these: "One part of matter can act upon another only by virtue of local motion, or, the effects and consequences thereof." —"For aught I can clearly discern, whatsoever is perform'd in the merely material world, is really done by particular bodies, acting according to the laws of motion." See Werkmeister, *A Philosophy of Science,* pp. 49-50.

48. A200/B245.

49. A200/B246; A202/B247. Despite the philosophical controversy over causality (since the days of Hume), the element of necessity implied in this formulation cannot be separated from the meaning of causal relations.

50. A202/B259.

51. This principle must not be misinterpreted as a principle of indeterminacy, as A. S. Eddington did in *The Nature of the Physical World* (1928), pp. 225, 309, 295.

52. Werner Heisenberg, *The Physical Principles of the Quantum Theory* (1930), pp. 3, 15. See also Kroebel, "Kant und die moderne Physik," p. 533: The cause of the uncertainty "liegt in dem Einfluss des Beobachtungsmittels bezw. des Beobachters auf das Messobjekt. Die Notwendigkeit der Begründung seiner Geltung zeigt damit bereits das Zugrundeliegen eines kategorialen Kausalverhältnisses an."

53. Werkmeister, *A Philosophy of Science,* pp. 274-77.

54. B256.

55. A216/B263.

56. A218/B266.

57. A323/B380.

58. A645/B672. But in no case does reason disclose the nature of the "thing-in-itself." Even the basic equations of modern quantum and wave mechanics do not do this. Werner Heisenberg put it this way: "Natural Science does not simply describe and explain nature; . . . it describes nature as exposed to our method of questioning." (*Physics*

and Philosophy: The Revolution in Modern Science. For his whole argument see: *Wandlungen in den Grundlagen der Naturwissenschaft;* Leipzig: Verlag S. Hirzel, 1935).

59. A644/B672.
60. Ibid.
61. A653/B681. A651/B679.
62. A697/B725.
63. A326/B383.
64. A328/B384.
65. Cf. Lothar Schäfer, "Zur 'Regulativen Funktion' der Kantischen Antinomien," *Synthesis: Kant and Modern Science* 23 (1) (1971): 96-120.
66. A423/B451.
67. A328/B384.
68. A426/B454.
69. Cf. Schäfer, "Zur 'Regulativen Funktion' . . ."
70. A434/B462.
71. See Dirac's thesis that our wave notion and our particle notion are but "two abstractions which are useful for describing the same physical reality." But we must not assume that wave and particles exist together in reality. Werkmeister, *A Philosophy of Science,* pp. 263f.
72. A665/B693.
73. A666/B694.
74. *Metaphysical Foundations of Natural Science,* translation and "Introduction" by James Ellington (Indianapolis: Bobbs-Merrill, Library of Liberal Arts, 1970). For a general commentary on this work see Lothar Schäfer, *Kants Metaphysik der Natur* (Berlin: Walter de Gruyter, 1966). My references will be to the Akademie-Ausgabe, Vol. 4, and to Ellington's translation (abbreviated E).
75. AA 4, 469; E, 5.
76. AA 4, 469; E, 6.
77. AA 4, 476f; E, 13f.
78. AA 4, 481; E, 19.
79. AA 4, 470. And: "A doctrine of nature will contain only so much science proper as there is applied mathematics in it." Ibid, p. 7.
80. AA 4, 487; E, 28. In chapter 4 Kant put it this way: "The rectilinear motion of a matter in no relation to matter outside of itself, i.e., such rectilinear motion thought of as absolute, is impossible." AA 4, 555; E, 120. And: "Absolute space is no object of experience and is nothing at all." AA 4, 556; E, 121.

81. Werkmeister, *A Philosophy of Science,* pp. 198-213. See also Alfred C. Elsbach, *Kant und Einstein* (Berlin: Walter de Gruyter, 1924), and Ernst Cassirer, *Zur Einsteinschen Relativitätstheorie: Erkenntnistheoretische Betrachtungen* (Berlin: 2d ed., 1921).

82. Werkmeister, *A Philosophy of Science,* p. 54. For a refutation of Newton's argument see ibid., pp. 56-58.

83. AA 4, 560; E, 127; AA 4, 561; E, 128.

84. AA 4, 561f; E, 128f.

85. AA 4, 562; E, 131.

86. Werkmeister, *A Philosophy of Science,* pp. 217-20.

87. Isaac Newton, *Opticks,* pp. 375-76. Cf. Werkmeister, *A Philosophy of Science,* p. 287.

88. Cf. Werkmeister, *A Philosophy of Science,* chapter 8: "The New Conception of Matter," pp. 229-77. —In any case, a reference to "ultimates" in this sense—be they "atoms" or "matter waves"—is but an inference from observations at the macrocosmic level.

89. Heisenberg, *Physics and Philosophy,* p. 48.

90. *Opus postumum* (Akademie-Ausgabe, Vols. XXI and XXII, hereinafter identified simply as I and II, indicating the line references in the usual way), I, 441, 30 – 442, 3; II, 212, 2–4.

91. I, 412, 8–9.

92. I, 579, 10–12; II, 269, 9–10; II, 324, 5–6.

93. AA 4, 503; E, 49.

94. AA 4, 497; E, 41.

95. AA 4, 497; E, 43.

96. AA 4, 501; E, 59.

97. AA 4, 508; E, 56, 57.

98. AA 4, 510; E, 59.

99. AA 4, 511; E, 60.

100. AA 4, 524; E, 77.

101. AA 4, 524; E, 78f. But the term "moving forces" must here not be taken in the mechanical sense of Newtonian physics.

102. II, 526, 22–23. For a different approach see Hansgeorg Hoppe, *Kants Theorie der Physik: Eine Untersuchung über das Opus postumum von Kant* (Frankfurt: Vittorio Klostermann, 1969).

103. I, 228, 24–5.

104. II, 523, 22–3.

105. I, 192, 15–20.

106. II, 475, 3–8; II, 421, 1–3.

107. I, 236, 15.

108. I, 224, 10–13.

109. II, 331, 1–2; II, 552, 5–7.
110. I, 218, 10–17; I, 236, 15–20; II, 475, 3–8; I, 542, 26–543, 11.
111. I, 584, 18–19; I, 589, 5–8; I, 602, 20–603, 2.
112. I, 581, 1–2; II, 612, 21–613, 4.
113. I, 553, 14–15.
114. I, 576, 7–9.
115. I, 217, 20–22.
116. I, 544, 12–15; I, 225, 12–15.
117. I, 424, 3–6.
118. II, 211, 23–5.
119. I, 444, 9–10; I, 593, 7–15; II, 275, 6–13.
120. Werkmeister, *A Philosophy of Science,* pp. 255–66.
121. von Weizäcker, "Kant's 'First Analogy . . .'," p. 93; I, 161, 15–22.
122. II, 371, 17–18; II, 391, 3; II, 358, 1–4; II, 400, 4–9; I, 510, 26–511, 2; I, 507, 1–2; and numerous other places.
123. I, 487, 22–3; I, 527, 18–19.
124. II, 340, 12–13.
125. II, 549, 18–28. Here again emerges the conception of the Great Chain of Being, to which Kant stood committed since 1755. See *Universal Natural History and Theory of the Heavens,* AA 1, p. 365; and the *Critique of Judgment,* AA 5, pp. 425-35.
126. I, 66, 2.
127. I, 60, 28–9; Cf. Werkmeister, *A Philosophy of Science,* pp. 325-34; 349-51.
128. I, 184, 10–13; I, 189, 6–10; I, 190, 4–5; I, 194, 12–21; I, 210, 24–5; I, 388, 11–18; and elsewhere. See also Walter B. Cannon, *The Wisdom of the Body* (New York: W. W. Norton & Co., 1932), p. 291: "The integrity of the organism as a whole rests on the integrity of the individual elements, and the elements, in turn, are impotent and useless save as parts of the organized whole."
129. I, 186, 7–12; I, 211, 10–15.
130. I, 194, 12-13; II, 285, 11-13, 24; I, 558, 15-20; II, 510, 9-11; II, 547, 2-5: "One can think of an organic body of nature as a natural machine, i.e., as a system of external moving forces which are internally combined into a system to which an idea is basic." See also Cannon, *The Wisdom of the Body,* p. 38 (quoting Claude Bernard, J. S. Haldane endorsing the idea): "All the vital mechanisms, however varied they may be, have only one object, that of preserving constant the conditions of life in the internal environment." And p. 249: "The preservation of constancy in the condition for free and independent life." And p. 279: "The operation of the system is such as to favor the welfare of the organism."

131. Professor Alfred Stern has called my attention to the fact that the French biologist Jacques Monod, winner of the Nobel Prize in Physiology and Medicine for 1965, came to the same conclusion. In *Le Hasard et la Nécessité* (Paris, 1970) he wrote (p. 60): "L'organisme est une machine qui se construit elle-même." The parallelism of the two statements is surely significant for an evaluation of Kant's position.
132. I, 196, 29-30.
133. I, 193, 13-18.
134. II, 356, 3-5; II, 499, 20-4; II, 501, 11-21.
135. II, 481, 8-10; II, 481, 13-17.
136. II, 548, 3-25.
137. II, 507, 1-10.
138. II, 271, 8-12.
139. Werkmeister, *A Philosophy of Science,* pp. 322–51, 362–65.

THE ROLE OF TELEOLOGY IN KANT'S WORK

Frederick P. Van De Pitte

In a recent article,[1] I have attempted to establish that Kant's distinction of judgments into "reflective" and "constitutive" is invalid by his own criteria. This fact would lend credence to the position asserted by several writers that Kant was wrong in assigning a mere subjective validity to teleology, the principle of reflective judgment. But one cannot ignore the fact that Kant had good reasons for drawing this distinction. I would like, therefore, to explore this area of Kant's thought, in order to determine what the effect would be on the Critical Philosophy as a whole if the function of reflective judgment were incorporated into his epistemology as a constitutive principle of the objective order of nature, rather than as one with merely subjective validity. And perhaps this can best be done by considering what might be lost, and what gained, if purposiveness were a constituent principle in Kant's epistemological scheme.

To begin with, there can be no doubt that Kant intended teleology to serve a vital function in his system. His statements in the introduction to the third *Critique* make the point very clearly that the notion of purposiveness can serve as both a formal and a real mediating principle with respect to the doctrines of the two earlier *Critiques*. But this mediation requires not merely the subjective and formal conception of purposiveness to be found in aesthetic judgments or in mathematical relationships. It requires, as well, the objective and real purposiveness which is the essential ingredient in our conception of organic objects and in our grasp of nature as an organized whole.[2]

It has been well argued by several writers that the doctrines thus advanced in the third *Critique* do not merely tie together the two otherwise disparate aspects of the Critical Philosophy. Rather, the doctrine of teleology first makes it possible to understand in a detailed manner the factors inherent in each of the previous works that Kant had either assumed, or left unnoticed, and in terms of which alone they could really deal effectively with their areas.[3] But the "mediating role" and the "supplementary role" of the third *Critique* should be dealt with separately.

One cannot fail to note the strain under which Kant is working when he asserts on the one hand that our conception of the organic object, or of nature as a whole, is impossible without the interpretive principle of purposiveness, and on the other, that this principle (as a principle of reflective judgment) is to be accorded *merely* subjective validity. The distinction between constitutive and regulative principles is, of course, *logically* valid. But is it legitimate in this context, and valid as applied? Clearly not. It is only necessary to recall that it forces Kant to assert an absolute and irreducible distinction between organic and inorganic nature—a position for which there is (and in principle *can be*) no critical justification. Kant is placed in the absurd position of asserting not only that we recognize a definite distinction between the two aspects of nature (in terms of his definitions), but, unaccountably, that it is impossible to reduce mechanical causality and causality through design to a single conceptual ground—or to reduce one to the other. This seems to be merely a dogmatic stand on Kant's part, and one which is incomprehensible in the "critical" role which he assumes for his system. It would obviously relieve this strain if purposiveness were, from the very beginning, a constituent element in his epistemological theory, and could function as a complementary interpretive principle with mechanical causality —never violating the latter, and always present to interpret aspects of nature which are otherwise opaque at a given time.[4]

Only in this way would Kant have the genuine mediation which he desires for his system. Obviously enough, if we grant that the power of judgment can legislate in terms of a priori principles for a certain aspect of human experience (feeling), the formal unity of the Critical Philosophy will be established. Kant will have dealt comprehensively with the a priori principles of nature through the understanding; the a priori principles of morality through reason; and the a priori principles which relate to feeling through reflective judgment. And since these faculties exhaust man's cognitive powers, in a sense the critical task is complete. But this would be a shallow achievement at best. Kant was not merely performing a formal gesture of filling out his technical system. He was attempting to demonstrate at the same time that the various kinds of experience open to man can and do "jell" into a comprehensive, organic whole. And this can only be achieved by permitting purposiveness to play an intrinsic part in both the epistemological and moral aspects of the Critical Philosophy. Something more is required to bring nature and morality into a coherent system than is provided in the first and second *Critiques*.

It is here that we begin to deal with the third *Critique* as supplementing, rather than merely mediating between the two earlier works, in an external manner. This can perhaps best be shown by pointing out that the role often assigned to the *Critique of Judgment*, as a more or less arbitrary unification of nature (causal necessity) and morality (causality through freedom), is inherently inadequate; and, moreover, that neither nature nor morality as Kant presents them is possible without assuming purposiveness in a constituent role. One may point out, for example, that the role reflective judgment plays in morality[5] (the projection of a unified scheme upon possible experience as a ground for the realization of the dictates of the moral law)[6] is perfectly adequate to serve the purposes of morality. But the merely subjectively valid evaluation of a moral position does nothing to assure one that it is actually possible to inject moral acts into the natural order: There are grounds for asserting that at the end of the second *Critique* Kant is by no means sure that he can offer more than the negative assurance (of the first *Critique*) that freedom and nature do not contradict each other. His emphasis upon the good will, rather than the achievement of the moral act, is surely relevant here. It is clear, however, that Kant *wanted* to provide assurance that man can affect the natural order through freedom—especially in the third *Critique*. As he asserts in the introduction (§ 2), the moral order, while absolutely distinct from the natural order, is *meant* to have an influence on the order of nature. And in the later pages of this work there is an enormous build-up of circumstantial evidence to provide the conviction that the world is indeed a context where purposes through freedom can be realized. But the evidence remains circumstantial, and reflective judgment remains only subjectively valid.

In once sense, we are dealing here simply with moral motivation, and Kant's position is psychologically sound if, in fact, cognitive powers such as ours *must* function in the way that he describes.[7] But can an ethical theory stand validly on the same ground? Must it not be clear in such a theory that it is at least *possible* to realize a moral act in the natural order?[8] If not, Kant's ethics would be open to the objection that perhaps we (as "morally free" entities) are merely spectators of the natural order, having no effect upon it, with morality consisting simply in the process of willing for or against events in our experiential field—which will occur as they occur whether we will or not.

This is, of course, a perversion of Kant's ethical scheme. But it must be acknowledged that reflective, teleological judgment, through which we must interpret nature as an order which is open to causality through design, can give us no knowledge to oppose such a misconstruction. Only if design is an intrinsic, constituent element of the natural order complementing blind mechanical causality can we be assured that causality through moral design (i.e., causality through freedom) is genuinely possible. Kant clearly desires the conclusion that such causality *is* possible, but he cannot justify it as his system is developed.

Moreover, to get at the heart of the matter, the theoretical philosophy cannot be made to work without purposiveness. This is clear in a minor sense when Kant asserts in the third *Critique* that we cannot know certain objects in nature, and that we cannot know nature as a whole, without the principle of design and teleological judgment. But a more precise, technical formulation of this principle in the context of the first *Critique* would have to answer some very difficult questions: Are the conditions for knowing a particualr object different from those required for a "unified experience as a whole"? And is not a given unified experience based precisely on a sense of "nature" as an organic whole (not worked out in detail, of course, but necessarily assumed)? Is it not also true that at least some inorganic natural objects cannot be properly understood without an organic conception? The distinction seems to be psychological, rather than logical, and one might well assert that no object can be fully understood without a conception of how the organic interplay of mechanical natural causes produced *this* object with *its* specific properties.

Indeed, just as careful studies have made clear the ingenuity displayed in Kant's argument (against Hume) that the very notion of 'event' presupposes causality, so one might demonstrate that 'object' is meaningless apart from the organic set of conditions within which an object of perception is possible. And the point, of course, is that while this organic unity is not essentially different from that specified in the third *Critique* as necessary for a grasp of nature as a whole, in the first *Critique* such a principle must be constitutive.

Kant's point, in effect, is that the sense of organic unity, which is a product of reflective judgment, is not reducible to the organic unity of the categories but is something more and merely regulative. On the contrary, however, if it is distinct from the categories, it is (like the transcendental unity of apperception itself) an essential precondition for the possible fulfillment or application of the categories. There can be no doubt that Kant understands the categories themselves to constitute an organic system. In fact, they form precisely the kind of system which he mentions in the "Architectonic of Pure Reason" (A832/B860): a system which can only be comprehended—as a whole, and in the relation of its parts—through the conception of its end, i.e., in this case, the unity of reflective consciousness in experience. And Kant maintains that such a system, like organisms themselves, can only be grasped through reflective judgment. Nor is this organic unity merely a characteristic of the abstract system of transcendental principles. It is essential to the concrete realization of these principles, as well.

Kant states clearly that the "thoroughgoing identity of the apperception of a manifold which is given in intuition contains a synthesis of representations, and *is possible only through the consciousness of this synthesis*" (B133, italics added). Merely empirical consciousness, he says, is scattered in that it accompanies different representations and lacks the essential relation to the identity of the subject. "That relation comes about not simply through my accompanying each representation with consciousness, but only insofar as I *conjoin* one representation with another, and am conscious of the synthesis of them." Then he concludes: "In other words, the analytic unity of apperception is possible only under the presupposition of a certain synthetic unity" (B133). One need only recall the more sophisticated aspects of Kant's epistemology, involving the synthesis of recognition in the Transcendental Deduction (A125-125). and reciprocity in the Analogies (A211/B257), to realize how extensive this synthesis is. And it should be clear that the unity of experience so constituted is precisely that of an organic system. This is the obvious significance of Kant's own statement with reference to the analogies: that, taken together, they assert "that all appearances lie in one nature, and must so lie, because without this a priori unity no unity of experience, and therefore no determination of objects in it, would be possible" (A216/B263). But this unity of experience, as organic, can only be the product of reflective judgment—and therefore it must be concluded that reflective judgment, and the principle of purposiveness on which it is based, play a constitutive rather than a merely regulative role in experience.[9]

In all fairness to Kant, one must register clearly his strong objection to the idea that purposiveness should be a constitutive principle of experience. He might first defend himself against the position emphasized by some writers, that while purposiveness is employed as a principle of knowledge which is only subjectively valid, this does not clearly distinguish it from other so-called "constitutive" principles. For, they point out, what Kant has established as the essential elements which alone can constitute the unity of apperception are also only subjectively necessary—in the sense that they are constitutive of objective knowledge for a subject of our kind. They are neither universal principles for knowledge of any sort in any kind of subject, nor objective in the sense that they establish anything about objective reality as such (things in themselves). But this objection is surely unsound. As noted above, the distinction between principles which reveal the essential order of nature (even as appearance), and one which only reveals the natural inclination of the subject to interpret that order, is at least logically valid and should not be attacked. Instead, it would be wiser to consider the essential issue involved: Precisely why has Kant chosen to employ this logical distinction, and what role does it ultimately play in his system?

In his earlier works, Kant had established to his own satisfaction the distinction between the sensible and intelligible worlds. His attempt to make room for faith by determining clearly the limits of knowledge was quite definitely an attempt to preserve the integrity of the moral order—though not in an arbitrary or artificial manner. But if purposiveness were given a constituent role along with mechanical causality, Kant would be confronted with a shift in the merely regulative role of the ideas of reason, and in effect one would be able to employ a teleological proof for the existence of God. As Beck has expressed it, "we should have the double absurdity of a theological physics and a theological morality."[10] For if the existence of God were established through speculative reason, morality (autonomy) would be reduced to an externally imposed heteronomous authoritarianism. Kant's opposition to such an ethical theory cannot be too strongly stated. On these grounds, he would be absolutely opposed to purposiveness as a constituent element of experience.

But is Kant's opposition well-grounded here? Would it really have been necessary for him to revise the table of categories, and to reopen the Pandora's box of rationalist metaphysics, in order to grant purposiveness a constitutive role in experience? I think not. It would be possible, for example, to conceive purposiveness as a third pure form along with space and time, which would serve as the ground for all levels of synthetic unity subsequently required in the Critical Philosophy. If this seems a curious notion at first, one need only recall the nature of space and time in the Aesthetic. They are nothing in themselves, yet serve as the essential conditions for empirical intuition. This role is clearly distinguished from the concept of space and time. At the level of perception, purposiveness would be the mere ground of affinity in terms of which an objective, ordered unity is possible in the manifold. And one should recall that the essential roles of space and time are to differentiate among contemporaneous and successive elements respectively. Is it not essential to ground, as well, the organic unity of these pure intuitions as constituting the "receptacle" of all experience? Purposiveness would thus serve as the ground for what Kant calls the "pure synthesis of apprehension" (A99-100).

It will be remembered that space and time are products of the imagination for Kant, and that the imagination is also the source of all synthesis in experience. Is it not reasonable to assert that the imagination, as the essential source of spontaneity in perception, not only could provide, but in fact requires, a principle of unification in terms of which this spontaneity can produce order? This would give greater significance to the concept of affinity—the ground of the unity of properties as *belonging* together in an appearance.[11] Kant clearly emphasizes that "the conditions of the *possibility of experience* in general are likewise conditions of the *possibility of the objects of experience*" (A157/B197). This does not mean, of course, that empirical objects are simply our consciousness of them. Rather, it means that there must be an empirical correlate for every transcendental principle of consciousness. I am suggesting, therefore, that the affinity of elements in an appearance which constitutes it an empirical unity is the objective correlate of the "pure form" of purposiveness through which the imagination expresses its inherently teleological operation.

One might suggest that since the imagination is an aspect of the understanding, the ground of the unity of its operation is identical with the unity of the understanding itself: the transcendental unity of apperception. But Kant says that "the principle of the necessary unity of pure (productive) synthesis of imagination, *prior to apperception,* is the ground of the possibility of all knowledge, especially of experience" (A118, my emphasis). If Kant is to maintain the distinctions that preserve him from pure idealism, he must account for a unity of appearances antecedent to the unity of experience which is consequent upon the application of the categories.

Nor is it reasonable for Kant to maintain, as he seems to at times (e.g., A107 and A110), that space and time can serve as the empirical ground of unity for appearances. For they require the synthesis of apprehension (grounded in a pure form of unity, I would maintain) for the possibility of their a priori representations (A99-100). Affinity is a better candidate for this task.

The advantages that Kant would gain by employing the revisions I suggest are important. There would be no necessity for a labored discussion of how it is that the cognitive powers work together harmoniously to construct a unified science. Reflective judgment would still serve its function, but in a determinant role which employed design along with mechanical causality (and its hypotheses would still require observation for confirmation, of course). But nature would now clearly be more receptive to the notion of causality through freedom—one level of design superimposed upon another, with no unbridgeable chasm between the two orders. And the enormous advantage for a unified conception of man's projected development toward the highest good would be hard for Kant to ignore.

Perhaps the most interesting aspect of the proposal, however, is that it would not cost Kant a great deal in his intentions for a Critical Philosophy. As a pure form of intuition, purposiveness would be valid only within the realm of empirical experience. It could not be used to establish anything about the noumenal order—either the *Ding-an-sich* or the existence of God. It would serve only as a unifying principle within experience. But it would provide, as well, an essential element which would justify the unacknowledged assumption of purposeful activity which one detects throughout the first *Critique.*

It would be appropriate to point out, perhaps, that although this revision of Kant's epistemology would be clearly heretical, it is at least not in violation of his own procedural norms. He says, for example:

> You know that I do not approach reasonable objec-
> tions with the intention merely of refuting them, but
> that in thinking them over I always weave them into
> my judgments, and afford them the opportunity of
> overturning all my most cherished beliefs.[1][2]

Since my suggestion would not overturn those beliefs, but
would perhaps support them more firmly, one might even hope
that Kant would approve the change. However, with or without
Kant's approval, the proposal has serious implications and must
be given serious consideration.

For example, even though the suggested revision might ultimately be judged untenable, the investigation involved in attempting to substantiate the position would involve such crucial
issues for Kant's system that it could not fail to throw new light
on essential problems. And if, on the other hand, teleology
could be given a transcendental justification as a constituent
element in Kant's epistemology, it would force us to reconsider
almost two centuries of the history and philosophy of science.
For the implication would be that nature is, and must be,
purposive as an object of human knowledge and investigation.

Not only would this revision provide Kant with an absolute
answer to Hume, and settle such issues as the problem of
induction. In addition, it would provide an insight into why
Pragmatism caught the attention of philosophers in the present
century, and point out the essential aspect which this move-
ment contributes to epistemology. And, of course, one might
also hope to find in this context the solution to such dilemmas
as that formulated by Jacques Monod in his recent work *Chance
and Necessity*. But these implications are too broad, and must
be worked out and dealt with in another context.

Surely someone will object at this point that this line of
thought involves too great a commitment for the simple hypothesis from which it is derived. After all, it is one thing to
attempt a revision of the structure of Kant's system in order to
strengthen it and render it more valid. It is quite another matter
to suggest that this valid system might also be *true*. But I am
very much impressed with the failure of recent attempts to
establish the impossibility of transcendental deductions in general, and to show the inadequacy of Kant's system in particular.

Moreover, one can hardly ignore the fact that Kant's thought is surprisingly compatible with contemporary scientific knowledge.[13] For these reasons, I would like to join Nicholas Rescher in his willingness to remain open-minded on the question of whether Kant's essential doctrines are to be rejected as false and obsolete. As he says:

> There is no reason why the Kantian doctrine of necessary truths of the synthetic *a priori* type should yet be buried—nobody is in a position to certify to its demise.[14]

The same might be said for other aspects of Kant's epistemological scheme, and in particular for the principle of purposiveness as an essential characteristic of human cognition. Whether this principle is subjectively necessary as Kant asserts, or objectively necessary as I have suggested, it is in either case "just as necessarily valid for our human judgment."[15] We have as yet no sound justification for rejecting this insight, and a careful examination of the place of teleology in Kant's system can only be enormously instructive for one who would attempt an objective evaluation of contemporary epistemological theories. We may yet find that our problems in epistemology lie not so much in a lack of progress in this field as in a failure to comprehend the insights long since achieved. In any event, Kant's thought on teleology is of far more than merely historical interest.

NOTES

1. "Is Kant's Distinction Between Reflective and Determinant Judgment Valid? in *Akten des 4. Internationalen Kant-Kongresses* (Berlin, 1974), pp. 445-51.
2. The groundwork for this study is provided by George Schrader's "The Status of Teleological Judgment in the Critical Philosophy." *Kant-Studien* 45 (1953-54): 204-35. However, since my conclusions are quite different, it would be wrong to imply that Schrader agrees with them.

3. In his *Die Teleologie in Kants Weltbegriff* (Bonn, 1968), Klaus Düsing provides an interpretation which displays man's need for both epistemological and moral teleology if he is to be truly oriented in the world.

4. As J. D. McFarland has pointed out, only if nature is in fact purposive for our understanding of it has Kant an answer to Hume—i.e., only in this way can he establish that empirical laws are ultimately necessary. Cf. *Kant's Concept of Teleology* (Edinburgh, 1970), p. 88.

5. Actually this process involves a complex interplay of both reflective and determinant judgment, as Lewis White Beck has noted in his commentary on the second *Critique*. Cf. *A Commentary on Kant's Critique of Practical Reason* (Chicago, 1966), p. 154n.

6. This moral teleology is distinguished by István Hermann as playing a vital role in Kant's system. *"Teleologie für sich"* (as distinct from physical teleology or *"Teleologie an sich"*) is the setting of goals by man in his projected moral development. This second aspect of teleology *(für sich)* Hermann calls the genuine *(eigentliche)* teleology. Cf. *Kants Teleologie* (Budapest, 1972), p. 315.

7. Kant's particular concern with the special nature of the human mind and the kind of necessity it imposes on our knowledge is dealt with by Nicholas Rescher in his "Kant and the 'Special Constitution' of Man's Mind," *Akten des 4. Internationalen Kant-Kongresses,* pp. 318-28.

8. It is not necessary that a particular act be a direct result of our willing it, but it is necessary that it be at least genuinely possible for us to effect such an act.

9. For a more extended discussion of this point see "Is Kant's Distinction Between Reflective and Determinant Judgment Valid? ," pp. 449-50. Max Leidtke has also provided an excellent analysis of issues related to this problem in "Der Begriff der reflektierenden Urteilskraft in Kants Kritik der reinen Vernunft" (Diss., Hamburg, 1964).

10. Leidtke, "Der Begriff . . .," p. 279.

11. This aspect of Kant's epistemology requires greater and more careful attention than can be provided here. However, it will perhaps suffice to point out that if the notion of affinity were consistently developed as the constitutive and objective ground of the synthetic unity of all experience, it would remove a great many difficulties for Kant. Certain of the categories would be more easily derived and more adequately grounded; the role of imagination and its task of providing synthetic unity could be made more intelligible; and indeed the whole notion of spontaneity could be made more meaningful.

12. Letter to Marcus Herz, June 7, 1771. AA 10, 116-17.
13. See, for example, the discussion of this matter by W. H. Werkmeister in the present volume.
14. "Kant and the 'Special Constitution' of Man's Mind," p. 328.
15. *Critique of Judgment,* § 76 to end.

KANT'S "COPERNICAN REVOLUTION"
AND THE CERTAINTY OF GEOMETRICAL KNOWLEDGE

Ted B. Humphrey

This paper deals with a crucial doctrine of Classical German
Idealism, the one Kant expresses when he writes that "reason
has insight only into that which it creates in accordance with its
own plan." My aim is to show that the sense of this insight in
Kant's thought is equivocal and that this fact leads to some
undesirable problems concerning his contentions about the certainty of at least some of our knowledge—problems he had
hoped to avoid by formulating critical idealism. To this end, I
shall examine two aspects of Kant's thought: (1) his conception
and preliminary defense of the Copernican revolution in philosophy, and (2) his conception of the necessity and certainty of
geometrical truth. The former sets out a very general strategy
for defending his new, non-Leibnizian theory of necessary,
certain propositions; I believe that one must understand that

The research for and the writing of this paper were done under a faculty
grant in aid from Arizona State University for Summer, 1973. I want to
thank the University and the Committee for their financial support of this
project.

strategy in order to comprehend fully Kant's theory of geometrical truth. On the other hand, the combination of Kant's accounts of (1) the source and the nature of man's cognitive relationship to (pure) spatial intuition and (2) geometrical method raises some problems for his theory of certainty in human knowledge. So far as I can determine, he never became aware of these problems. Just how much bearing they may have on his general theory or for his theory as it applies to other kinds of knowledge, such as arithmetical, physical or critically metaphysical knowledge, I have not yet been able to determine. Careful examination shows, however, that Kant's conclusions about space and geometry tended to precede by at least a year, and often more, his other theories, including his most general one, about human knowledge. Further, important analogies exist between the theories concerning space and geometry and those regarding knowledge in general or other specific fields of knowledge. Thus, my conclusions about the Copernican revolution and geometrical knowledge may have more general consequences.

Kant prefaced the second edition of the *Kritik der reinen Vernunft* with an extended analogy concerning method and the turn of events whereby areas of investigation become scientific. The parts of this analogy that have received the most attention, particularly among English-writing students of Kant's thought, refer to Copernicus. Scholars generally hold that Kant maintains that his approach does for epistemology and metaphysics—at least as a natural disposition—what Copernicus's theory did for man's ordinary conception of apparent cosmic motions, namely, make them a function of the motion, position, and nature of the observer rather than of the observed *simpliciter* (Bxii, n.).[1] The normal reason for discussing this analogy is to determine precisely what Kant meant by it and whether, so understood, it is accurate.[2] Such an approach concentrates on only a very small portion of its total content. Although I believe the analogy does provide a clue to the fundamentally new standpoint of Kant's critical epistemology and metaphysics, this aspect of the total discussion does not strike me as particularly important. Far more crucial is the issue of how the opening paragraphs of the second edition Preface (Bvii-xxiv) serve as an initial justification for Kant's critical idealism and the conception of necessity and certainty inherent in it. I shall discuss this in the first major division of the paper. In the second, I shall take up Kant's defense of the necessity and certainty of geometrical knowledge.

1

A. The background of the second edition Preface. The principle underlying critical idealism is that "reason has insight only into that which it creates in accordance with its own plan" (Bxiii). While this view clearly permeates the first edition of the *Kritik,* as well as the *Prolegomena,* Kant never explicitly states it in either. Prior to preparing the second edition, he apparently did not become clearly aware of it as constituting one of the premises underlying the general strategy of his arguments; instead it lay implicit in his mind, taking the form of a hidden premise of his thought.[3] The premise was undoubtedly at the back of Kant's mind from the time he began to write the central portions of his critical epistemology, for he at least hints at it in the first edition Preface (Axx) but does not elaborate on it and fails to use it in the comments preceding section 1 of the *Prolegomena.*[4]

The fundamental purpose of the portion of the second edition Preface that concerns us is to determine what constitutes the essence of the change in outlook and investigative procedure by means of which an area of investigation becomes scientific.[5] In the first half of the section, Bvii-xv, Kant analyzes bodies of knowledge that have already become scientific and in the second half, Bxv-xxiv, he applies the results of this analysis, by means of an argument by analogy, to metaphysics. In setting up his model, Kant first cites three criteria that allow one to determine whether an area has entered on the "secure path of a science." Although these criteria are not sufficient to determine if an area actually has become scientific, they are adequate, as Kant notes at Bxiv, to show that metaphysics as practiced by his predecessors and contemporaries has not entered the "secure path of a science." Immediately following the introductory paragraph and taking up the rest of this first section is an analysis of the three fields that have, in Kant's opinion, actually become scientific, namely, logic, geometry, and natural science. Kant's analysis of these fields begins with the one that earliest in its practice became scientific and that he regards as intrinsically most scientific, i.e., logic, and concludes with the one that is intrinsically least scientific, because least self-contained, natural science.

B. *Kant's development of the model.* Of the three fields Kant uses to set up the model for his analogy, logic is the only one he appears to believe has not undergone—because it did not really have to—the revolution he intends to make in epistemology and metaphysics. He writes, logic is a "science . . . that completely displays and rigorously proves nothing except the formal rules of all thought" (Bix). Man's success in making a science of logic is due entirely to the fact that the logician "is bound to abstract from all objects and their differences; consequently, in logic the understanding has to deal solely with itself and its form" (Bix).

Given the immediate context of these remarks, Kant is certainly expressing the belief that logic deals only with those fundamental, indispensable rules and principles in accordance with which a finite rational creature must consider any set of facts or propositions.[6] Thus, he takes it as given that logic is a strictly a priori science that serves as a propaedeutic to all other investigations.[7] The reasons he gives for its apriority is that its exclusive source is the mind, and that it is the conceptual expression of man's intrinsic capacity for ratiocinative activity. Kant's contentions in this discussion of logic depend on a strong but never clearly expressed and analyzed relation in his thought between what I shall refer to in the ensuing discussion as genetic apriority and logical apriority.

The notion of genetic apriority applies primarily to the sources of representations *(Vorstellungen)*[8] rather than to representations themselves. For while Kant wants to avoid all theories of innate ideas, i.e., occurrent representations that are a priori and yet not dependent on the nature or inherent dispositions of the (human) mind, he does hold that dispositions[9] not acquired from empirical stimulation produce representations. Thus, we can say that a disposition, or an occurrent representation that has such a disposition as its source, is genetically a priori if (a) its exclusive basis is the mind or one of its faculties, i.e., if, in Kant's terminology, it lies "prepared beforehand" *(vorbereitet)* in the mind; and if (b) it can, if it is a disposition, function independently of, though not necessarily prior to, all empirical stimulation of the cognitive capacities or, if it is an occurrent representation, be made present to consciousness independently of any arbitrarily chosen empirical object of consciousness, even if it cannot be present altogether devoid of such content; and if (c) given that it is a disposition, it plays an essential role in the constitution (organization) of at least some class of the possible objects of consciousness, or, if it is an occurrent representation, occurrent empirical objects of consciousness are organized within or organizable in accordance with it.[10] The notion of logical apriority applies primarily to occurrent representations, and we can say that a representation is logically a priori vis-à-vis another representation when it is logically presupposed or entailed by that representation. Kant maintains that some representations are absolutely logically prior to at least some large classes of the occurrent objects of consciousness. These include space, time, the "I think," the pure forms of judgment and the categories. That, according to Kant, these logically a priori occurrent representations have genetically a priori dispositions as their sources is an important point for this discussion. Kant's characterization of logic in the second edition Preface makes this point nicely. For while logic may consist of a set of rules that can be present to consciousness as occurrent representations, the certainty and completeness of logic stem from the fact that those rules merely display discursively the strictly formal nature of the understanding, which we can conceive as a disposition to organize, under certain conditions and in specific ways, the occurrent objects of consciousness, be they pure or empirical.

If logic required no revolution in order to become scientific, geometry, as well as the rest of mathematics, certainly did. Early on, mathematical investigations had the character of mere *Herumtappen* that, according to Kant, presently affects metaphysics. But at some unrecorded date, a revolution in mathematical method *(Revolution der Denkart)* occurred:

> A light flashed upon the mind of the first person who demonstrated the properties of the isosceles triangle for he found that he did not learn its characteristics from what he saw in the figure or what he

> deduced from the concept of it; but he had to pro-
> duce (by construction) what he had himself, accord-
> ing to concepts a priori, placed and represented in the
> figure, so that, in order to know anything with cer-
> tainty, he could not attribute to it anything except
> what follows from what he placed in it in accordance
> with that concept. (Bxii)

The transition by means of which geometry became scientific
was the introduction of an a priori element into it, one that has
its source in the self-motivated thinking activity of the
knower.[11] Now in this analysis of the revolution in geometry,
the confusion between genetic and logical apriority does not
arise. Instead, another form of apriority is used to explain the
change, a form that resembles the one found in practical knowledge, in which concepts antedate the existence of their objects[12] (AA 5, 171-3). Kant's characterization of the change
emphasizes the temporal and logical priority of the concept in
relation to the construction of an object about which one
desires to formulate propositions. Those propositions must be
formulated on the basis of observing the properties of an object
constructed in accordance with the concept. Kant characterizes
mathematical concepts as comprising the minimal necessary and
sufficient rules for constructing an object of a certain sort. This
theory, that concepts formulated through self-motivated thinking activity constitute a unique a priori element in mathematics,
does not make up Kant's entire critical doctrine of mathematical knowledge, but it is a crucial independent element of it.[13]

The revolution in the empirical part of natural science closely
resembles the one in geometry, and Kant describes it in similar
terms. A revelation came to the early practitioners of experimental method:

> They grasped that reason has insight only into that
> which it creates in accordance with its own plan and
> that it must not allow itself to be tied by nature's
> tethers, but proceed with principles of judgment
> based on fixed laws, constraining nature to answer its
> questions. Reason with its principles in one hand
> according to which alone concordant appearances can

be admitted as equivalent to laws, and in the other its experiments that it has devised in conformity with these principles, must approach nature to be taught by it, not, however, with the attitude of a pupil but of a judge who compels witnesses to answer the questions he has formulated. (Bxiii)

Experimental method in natural science, as Kant here describes it, involves the same kind of a priori element as mathematics, namely, a concept or proposition, an hypothesis, that is the product of self-motivated, spontaneous reflection on nature, on the basis of which one performs experiments in order to determine whether nature actually conforms with it. Experimental method is not solely inductive, for while hypotheses may be inductively tested, their sole criteria of adequacy are not inductively obtained, nor are they formulated solely on the basis of induction.[14] For Kant the single most important element in the revolution of empirical science is the self-motivated, spontaneous act of hypothesis and experiment formation, not because it antedates encounter with the world, but rather because one can control and be fully and explicitly aware of the content of propositions expressing hypotheses and experimental procedure. This is precisely what he means when he writes, "They grasped that reason has insight only into that which it creates in accordance with its own plan."

Kant's concept of the hypothetico-experimental method not only provides a confirmation procedure, but also involves essentially an element for which man as knower is not dependent on the material conditions of existence, namely, the specific content of the conceptual element that is the product of the thinker's self-motivated, spontaneous activity. Only in respect to the products of such activity can (finite) thinkers have insight *(Einsicht)* because only these products are fully subject to control of their content by their formulators. The important feature of mathematical concepts and scientific hypotheses is that man as knower stands in an active relationship to them, imbuing them with content, rather than a cognitively passive relationship, where he is dependent for the content of concepts on the material conditions of existence and genetic conditions of cognition. This unique relationship to some of the contents of mathematical and scientific knowledge Kant finds to be a necessary condition for the element of cognitive certainty and constant progress that those areas of investigation display.

C. Kant's application of the model to metaphysics. Given the impressive results achieved in logic, mathematics and natural science, Kant is dismayed by the present state of metaphysics. On the one hand, it is "a wholly isolated, purely speculative form of rational knowledge that rises completely above the ability of experience to instruct and in which reason must be its own student"; on the other hand, it has not entered the "secure path of a science." Indeed, it meets none of the necessary conditions of scientificness enumerated in the Preface's opening paragraphs. Thus, Kant suggests:

> The examples of mathematics and natural science, which have become what they now are through a single, sudden revolution, are sufficiently remarkable that one feels compelled to determine whether the essential aspects of the alteration in method that proved so fruitful in their instances, might not be experimented with in metaphysics, at least so far as an analogy qua forms of rational knowledge exists between the former and the latter areas of investigation. (Bxvi)

On the basis of an analogy, Kant intends to determine whether the "revolution in method" that proved so useful in altering the status of mathematics and natural science might apply to metaphysics. However, the analogy between the two kinds of investigations is just that, an analogy, and that is why Kant adds the important proviso that the revolutionizing insight in mathematics and natural science can apply to metaphysics only insofar as all three are forms of rational knowledge *(Vernunfterkenntnisse).* Of course, metaphysics is far more a form of rational knowledge than either natural science or mathematics, and this, we shall see, underlies some differences in the revolutionizing process that took place in the latter areas and the one that must be instituted in metaphysics. These differences are basic and crucial.

Kant's proposal for metaphysics is precisely this:

> One should experiment, then, whether we might not proceed better in the tasks of metaphysics were we to assume that objects must conform to our mode of cognition, which better than any other theory conforms with our desire to possess a priori cognition of objects. If intuition must conform to the nature of objects, it is impossible for me to comprehend how one might know them a priori. However, if they (as objects of the senses) conform to our capacity for intuition, then I can fully understand this possibility. (Bxvi-xvii)

This passage expresses the alternatives that Kant believes are open to him, and the one with which he will experiment comprises what is generally regarded as the Copernican revolution in metaphysics. The crucial issues concerning Kant's hypothesis are (1) the basis for his initial feeling of justification in suggesting it, (2) the precise meaning of his suggestion, and (3) the means by which he believes it can be verified. I shall deal with them in that order.

(1) Kant had already effected a Copernican revolution with respect to the fundamental principles of sensuous awareness in 1770, when, without using the *Kritik*'s terminology, he argued that space and time are pure forms of outer and inner intuition and empirically real, though transcendentally ideal. The second major step came when, dissatisfied with the account of pure concepts he had given in *De mundi sensibilis atque intelligibilis forma et principiis,* he expressed to Herz in the letter of February 21, 1772, that he could not accept concept empiricism, the view that man possesses only an *intellectus ectypi,* the doctrine of innate ideas, which he regarded as an appeal to a *deus ex machina,* or the view that the mind creates objects by acts of understanding, i.e., the view that the mind is an *intellectus archetypi* (AA 10, 124-26). Kant first expressed his basic solution to the problem of a priori conceptual knowledge in 1774–75, when he wrote that there "... *können dem Verstande keine andere Begriffe beiwohnen, als welche auf die*

Disposition und die Ordnung unter dieser Anschauung gehen"
(AA 17, 640). One should note two things about these early
developments. First, Kant never abandoned his rejection of the
three views regarding the relation of pure concepts to objects, at
least not when they are attributed to man. One finds his
dissatisfaction with them reiterated in whole or in part at
A92/B125–A93/B126, B167-8, and in *loses Blatt* C 8 (AA 18,
272-75). Second, seeming almost to pick up at the point at
which the discussion concerning the relation of pure concepts
of objects ends in the Herz letter and cognate passages, the
second edition Preface merely expresses the view that one must
make a new attempt to explain the relation.

(2) The very *crux* of Kant's newly proposed view, his "revolution in method" in metaphysics is in the following passage:

> Experience is itself a form of cognition that requires
> understanding, and I must, therefore, before objects
> are ever given to me, presuppose the rules of under-
> standing as existing within me a priori, these rules
> being expressed in a priori concepts, in accordance
> with which all objects of experience must agree and
> necessarily conform. (Bxvii-xviii)

Kant's contention about the apriority of pure concepts of
understanding is strikingly different from the one regarding
mathematical concepts and scientific hypotheses. He never argues, nor can he, that experience *must conform (übereinstim-
men müssen)* with the latter, whereas it must with the former.
In geometry and natural science, the issue of conformity is
determined by construction in presented space and experimentation and remains *thus far* contingent on the metric properties
of that space or upon those of experientially encountered
objects. For pure concepts of understanding, as well as for the
pure forms of intuition, the conformity is necessary, and the
issue of confirmation *in the relevant way* cannot arise.[15]

The difference between the relation of pure concepts (and
pure intuition) and mathematical concepts and scientific hypotheses to the field of human awareness is crucial. Central to
the difference is the relation in which man as knower stands to
the two kinds of concepts. In mathematical and scientific

thought the knower qua thinker is self-motivating in relation to the a priori element. As self-motivated thinker, he actually gives the content to the concept he wants to construct or to the hypothesis he wants to confirm. But in relation to pure concepts (and intuitions), particularly insofar as they are either dispositions or products of dispositions, man as knower is not active; as self-motivated thinker he does not imbue them with their nature and content. Instead, they constitute the structural basis of man's ability to be aware perceptually, conceptually, cognitively and aesthetically[16] of what there is. This view of Kant's, that man as knower exercises no control over the content of pure concepts and intuitions, becomes apparent in the last quotation, where he states that the rules to which experience must conform are *in* one—he actually says *in mir* —before any object can be given to one and that they are *therefore* a priori. The pure concepts and intituitions, either as dispositions or as occurrent representations produced by those dispositions, are, with respect to their nature and content, constitutive of man's ability to perceive, think, and cognize and hence cannot be products of man's self-motivated thinking activity. They may very well be presupposed by human experience, but that is precisely because they are genetically a priori, viz., dispositions, or the pure products thereof, that are constitutive of man's cognitive capacity.

The motivating insight of the critical epistemology and metaphysics is that, "we assume as the altered method of thought that we know a priori about things only what we put into them" (Bxviii). This kind of talk should now have a familiar ring because Kant used it twice earlier, though in somewhat different forms, to describe the revolution by means of which mathematics and natural sciences became scientific. However, in this third use, its meaning is drastically changed. The change results from an ambiguity in the terms *"mir"* and *"wir,"* which in the paradigm cases of geometry and natural science refer to the self-motivated thinker, but which with respect to pure concepts and intuitions refer to the very constitution of man's cognitive capacities. The foregoing considerations justify two contentions: (a) The very proposal of the Copernican revolution in metaphysics is not only embedded in a greater context, as I claimed at the outset, but is also based on an analogy that the sources of pure concepts and intuitions are supposed to have with the concepts in other areas of investigation. (b) However, the relevant aspects of the paradigms Kant uses to establish the model for the analogy are crucially different from those in pure concepts and intuitions.

(3) Kant refers to his Copernican hypothesis as an experiment in metaphysics that requires confirmation. He seems to recognize that a sufficient difference exists between mathematics and natural science on the one hand and pure concepts and intuitions on the other, so that he feels compelled to discuss in general terms the method he will use to confirm his hypothesis about the latter. Mathematical concepts and scientific hypotheses can be confirmed directly by subjecting them to the constructive and experimental process. The situation is quite different with pure concepts and intuitions, just because they either are dispositions or are the products of dispositions. They cannot be formulated and brought by the self-motivated thinker to what presents itself as experience because they constitute the very conditions without which what is presented either as perception, thought or cognition could not have the character it, in fact, does have. However, the concept of the *Copernican hypothesis itself can be subjected to a kind of experiment.* Kant proposes that it be proven indirectly, by *reductio ad absurdum,* his favorite form of argumentation.

Kant cannot directly disprove the dogmatists' position because it requires that one do what Kant claims is impossible, deal directly with things-as-they-are-in-themselves. In order to demonstrate the truth of his position, Kant must assume that concept empiricism and the doctrine of innate ideas are the only dogmatic theories of the concepts possessed by the understanding, and that his distinction between dogmatic and critical metaphysics is exhaustive and mutually exclusive. He must then show that his account of the sources and nature of pure concepts and intuitions provides an internally consistent theory of (a) the necessary and yet synthetic propositions of human knowledge and (b) metaphysics as a natural disposition, whereas dogmatic metaphysics either fails to provide a theory of necessary synthetic knowledge or is inherently antinomic (Bxix-xx, cf. AA 10, 336-43).

In a note, Kant comments that the method he uses in demonstrating the truth of his Copernican hypothesis resembles the method of chemists who, by extracting certain portions from a compound and recombining them, determine the compound's nature and necessary constituents (Bxx n.). This is a clear attempt to arouse the belief that the problems of confirmation confronted and the methods used by metaphysicians are very similar to the natural scientist's. But the analogy remains incomplete because natural scientists are able to effect a separation of elements that the metaphysician is not (AA 8, 119 n.). The metaphysician is constrained to adopt an indirect method of proof for his conception of the origin and scope of pure concepts.

All of this clarifies the role Kant understands the Transcendental Dialectic to play in the *Kritik*. The Dialectic is necessary to providing the truth of the Copernican hypothesis, and it is not, as is commonly believed, attached as an afterthought to the first half of the *Kritik* either to provide some cash value for what has gone before or to make the architectonic complete. Kant writes:

> The metaphysician's analysis separates pure a priori cognition into two quite heterogenous elements, namely things as appearances and things-in-themselves. His Dialectic combines these two again, to make them harmonious with the necessary rational idea of the unconditioned, and finds that his putative harmony can never be maintained, except through the above distinction, which must therefore be supposed to be true. (Bxxi n.)

The first half of the *Kritik,* to A293/B349, constitutes the full explication of the Copernican hypothesis concerning intuitions and concepts, the "deduction of our capacity to know a priori." By itself, it does not constitute a proof of the thesis. Without the Dialectic, the first half of the *Kritik* would remain a mere conception of the nature and scope of those representations alternative to the dogmatists', lacking all proof. By showing that the dogmatic account of pure concepts is essentially antinomic,

Kant indirectly proves the truth of the Copernican hypothesis. Thus, the Dialectic plays an indispensable role in motivating Kant to formulate the Copernican hypothesis, as he claims in the letter to Garve (AA 12, 257-8) and in demonstrating its truth. What I now want to do is examine the adequacy of Kant's Copernican conception of the origin and nature of pure concepts and intuitions in order to determine if, in fact, it can guarantee the certainty of our knowledge. The case that I shall examine is the certainty of geometrical knowledge afforded by Kant's system, a case with respect to which he was quite confident.

2

A. Kant's doctrine of the nature of geometrical knowledge. All but two of the main elements of Kant's doctrine of the nature and sources of geometrical knowledge that appear in the *Kritik* were formulated by 1770. These include his views on the nature of properly geometrical method, the genetically a priori origin of space (and time), and that geometrical knowledge is a priori. By 1775 he had developed the further views that geometrical propositions are synthetic and that they apply necessarily to all man's knowledge of things insofar as they can appear to him in outer intuition, a doctrine that is made particularly strong by virtue of the fact that he had by then also decided that *all* man's knowledge necessarily involves a sensuously intuitive element, a change from the doctrine of 1770.[17] Even though he had formulated all of its main features by 1775, his theory of geometrical knowledge is scattered throughout the *Kritik,* appearing partially in the Introduction, partially in the Aesthetic, partially in the (second edition) Analytic and partially in the "Transcendental Doctrine of Method." My first task, then, shall be briefly to present it here as a whole, concentrating especially on Kant's contentions regarding its necessity and certainty.

The most comprehensive statement concerning geometrical knowledge is in the second paragraph of the "Transcendental Exposition of the Concept of Space":

> Geometry is a science that determines the characteristics of space synthetically and yet a priori. . . . The

representation of space must originally be an intuition because from a mere concept one can obtain no propositions that go beyond the concept, which certainly occurs in geometry. This intuition must also be a priori, i.e., it must be found in us before all perception of an object, and must therefore be pure, not empirical intuition. For geometrical propositions are all apodictic, that is, bound up with the consciousness of their necessity. . . . (B40-1)

This paragraph contains references to three doctrines not adequately explicated in it.

The first is that geometrical knowledge can be regarded as a priori just because its propositions are reports about the metric of a space that—while serving as a formal, necessary condition appertaining to the cognitive subject to be affected by a certain class of objects—can be made present to consciousness as an occurrent representation independently of any affection of sensibility.[18] Consequently, one central element of Kant's theory of the certainty of geometrical knowledge is that occurrent representations of space are genetically a priori, at least insofar as they have their source in a disposition—i.e., outer sense—through which what is given by affection of sensibility is given a spatial form that can function independently of the affection of sensibility.[19]

The second doctrine this passage contains is that properly geometrical propositions are synthetic, in addition to being a priori. Kant writes that "necessity and strict universality" are the criteria of a priori propositions (B4) or that they are, in terms of the foregoing extended quote, "apodictic, i.e., bound up with the consciousness of their necessity" (cf. A713/B741). The syntheticity of geometrical propositions is a function of the fact that none can be known to be true of the space men apprehend by means of its conceptual expression alone. Figures displaying the relations attributed to spatial concepts must be constructible within that space in order to verify the truth-value of propositions about those relations. This feature of the synthetic apriority of geometrical propositions does not worry me so much as the other, i.e., the necessity and certainty that are a function of their apriority. And even here, necessity does not bother me, at least so far as one grants Kant his theory that space and time are necessary conditions of human sensuous awareness (A24/B38-9; A31/B46). However, Kant's contentions about certainty are perplexing. A great deal of the source of the worry is located in "apodictic," which in Kant's lexicon carries connotations of both necessary and certain. In the foregoing quotation he makes certainty a function of necessity. That is, what is necessary can be known with certainty (AA 4, 280). Whether this doctrine can be held, at least given Kant's other doctrines concerning space (and time), will be the major topic of section B of this part of my paper.

Kant's third essential doctrine concerning geometry is methodological. Geometry uses constructive method:

> Mathematical cognition is cognition by means of construction of concepts. By constructing a concept I mean representing an a priori intuition corresponding to it. For the construction of a concept, then, a *nonempirical* intuition is required, which, consequently, as intuition, is a *single* object, but which, as the construction of a concept, must have universal validity for all possible intuitions that fall under the concept. Thus I construct a triangle by representing the object corresponding to that concept either by mere imagination, in pure or, alternatively, on paper in empirical intuition. In both instances, however, this has been done entirely a priori, without having borrowed the model from experience. (A713/B741; A791/B819–A792/B820)

The theory that properly mathematical method is constructive is the earliest, and, so far as I can see, an independent element of Kant's doctrine of geometrical knowledge. Constructive method is a means of determining whether an object corresponds to a concept, e.g., the concept of the two-sided enclosed figure, and what facts may be true about such concepts, e.g., whether the interior angles of a triangle are equal to, greater, or less than 180 degrees. In the *Prize Essay,* where Kant first formulated the method, he ascribed all the certainty and progress of mathematics to its use of this method (AA 2, 291-2).

The essential element that it introduces into mathematics, as I noted earlier, and as Kant states in the final sentence of the foregoing quote, is a concept that arises as a function of the self-motivated thinking activity of the mathematician and which he brings to space and time for the construction of an object so that he can determine whether it has a reference and, if so, what its properties are. Thus, one can see that Kant's philosophy of geometry involves appeal to two quite different kinds of a priori elements, the genetically a priori origin of space and time and the self-motivated acts of thought that produce concepts independently of experience. What we must now determine is just what each of these elements contributes to Kant's doctrine of the certainty of geometrical knowledge.

B. The problem of certainty of Kant's doctrine of geometrical knowledge. A passage from the *Prolegomena,* one that has a correlate in the second edition of the *Kritik,* raises very nicely the problem of the roles that the doctrines of the genetically a priori origin of space and the self-motivately a priori origin of mathematical concepts play in geometrical knowledge.

> Space is something so homogeneous and in respect of all particular properties so indeterminate that there is certainly no treasure of natural laws to be found in it. On the other hand, that which determines space into the figure of a circle, cone and sphere is the understanding insofar as it contains the ground of the unity of the construction of these figures. The mere universal form of intuition called space is certainly the substratum of all intuitions that can be designated particular objects, and admittedly there lies in space the condition of the possibility and variety of the latter. However, the unity of objects is determined solely by the understanding and, indeed, according to conditions lying in its intrinsic nature. (AA 4, 321-22)[20]

Space as mere form of intuition, i.e., as pure manifold and hence as a mere determinable, contributes, according to this account, absolutely nothing to one's knowledge of its metric properties. Discovery of metric is a function of a knower's act of formulating a concept and attempting to construct it in that merely determinable manifold. If that is the case, what role can the fact that space is a pure form of intuition play in guaranteeing certainty to geometrical knowledge? To serve such a function it must stand as an independent determinate something, not as a mere determinable one. I think that were one to hold Kant to the letter of what he writes here, one would have to conclude that the intuited properties of figures constructed in accordance with a concept would be a function of conceptualization, of an expectation of intuiting a particular measure property, rather than of the instrinsic measure properties of presented space, assuming it had any. Consequently space as a pure form of intuition would not serve as an independent criterion of the truth value of concepts and propositions about space's metric. But this is not the main line of criticism I want to pursue.[21]

Kant's theory of geometrical method secures a guarantee that geometry has a particular kind of truth in which he was very much interested, namely, that its concepts and propositions have a reference. But his theory of space is supposed to assure that those referents have a specific presentational content that limits what can be expressed discursively in a judgment about them. We must question to what extent Kant's theory of the nature and origin of space can serve as the basis for determining *with certainty* the presented content of the putative referents of geometrical concepts and propositions.

Kant's theory of geometrical method is not dependent on any particular metaphysical theory about the origin of space. One could quite plausibly hold, as he seemed to in 1747 and 1763, that all man's knowledge of space is empirical—because it exists independently of the mind as an order obtaining among things-in-themselves—and still argue that properly geometrical knowledge of space is possible only if one employs constructive method. In that case, attempts at construction would be quite similar to experiments in that by means of them one would be attempting systematically to discover what the metric of space is. Nevertheless, the force behind the activity would consist of the self-motivatedly a priori formulations of geometrical concepts, axioms and propositions. One would be, in that regard, cognitively active in mathematical investigation.

Claims for the certainty of geometrical propositions by an empiricist using Kant's method would probably not be well received, for they would be regarded as merely contingent, empirical propositions. Two considerations very generally militate against attributing cognitive certainty to empirical propositions. These are, first, the standard Humean objections, along with their refinements, against induction. And second, we can never be absolutely certain that we have completely and accurately apprehended what is presented to us merely empirically. (This is rather more a Bayleian than a Humean objection.) Kant subscribes to these doubts about our apprehension of the empirical elements of what is intuitively presented, and since I believe that these problems with the empirical can be presented more abstractly, they may well be brought to bear on Kant's theory of the role of the pure manifold of space in geometrical knowledge.

Receptivity is the essential characteristic of a finite knower's—i.e., man's—relation to the empirical. The empirical, even for Kant, is something that men cannot control merely insofar as they are knowers. Instead, they stand in a receptive relation to it, and that prevents them from asserting with certainty that (1) they have not mistakenly apprehended a particular state of affairs and (2) particular states of affairs shall obtain in the future.[22] Thus, even though an empiricist might well be tempted to adopt Kant's theory of geometrical method, he would still be debarred from claiming cognitive certainty for his contentions about space's metric, because an essential part, indeed, the very foundation, of his epistemology is the claim that man is cognitively receptive to the content of knowledge.

An object lesson so far as Kant's views are concerned can be garnered from the empiricist's problems regarding certainty. From 1770 on, Kant separated his doctrine about human intuition into two parts, a doctrine of empirical intuition and a doctrine of pure sensuous intuition, presupposed by the former. In both he insists that to say that human intuition is sensuous means that man as knower stands in a passive or receptive relation to what is given intuitively. Space and time are given to men as knowers as intuitions; they are also forms of human sensibility, which in turn is just man's capacity for standing in a receptive relation to, or being affected by, objects so that *they* can be "given" to him (A19/B33). This, really, is the substance of Kant's claim that space and time are empirically real, for by that he means that, even as pure intuitions, men as knowers stand in a passive relationship to space and time. Indeed, did they not, it would be exceedingly difficult to explain why it took so long to generate a theory like Kant's about the origin of space and why persons tend to find it goes so much against the ordinary point of view.

The theory of space's empirical reality is conjoined with the doctrine of its transcendental ideality, which is, in the final analysis, the expression of Kant's view that space has a genetically a priori origin. Kant is able to make plausible his contention that space is empirically real and yet transcendentally ideal only because he ultimately appeals to its deep-seated, essentially uncontrollable origin in man's metaphysical constitution. Men as knowers are not active in the generation of space, even though it may have a genetically a priori origin in outer sense or in productive imagination. Man's metaphysical nature is not something he can control, at least not in the relevant sense.

Thus, in his theory of geometrical knowledge, Kant similarly to the empiricist who might adopt his method, has two quite disparate elements. On the one hand, he holds that in properly mathematical activity men play an active role as self-motivated formulators of the concepts and propositions to be constructed. On the other, men as knowers are merely passive observers of the media in which the construction is made. Man's position vis-à-vis space on Kant's analysis is genuinely analogous to that of the empiricist's. And given it, Kant is beset with the crucial problem of cognitive passivity, namely, the possibility of misapprehending what has been constructed and is presentationally before consciousness. This is devastating for Kant because all real, as opposed to merely nominal, content of mathematical knowledge derives from what one intuits as the determinate measure properties of an occurrent spatial representation given in intuition through the act of construction.

Kant's theory of the self-motivatedly a priori concept and proposition in geometry provides an element over which men have complete control and of the content of which they can therefore be certain. One can reasonably say that one can have complete insight into their content because they are stipulative products of the knower's activity. But his demand that in order for such a concept or proposition to have a determinate truth-value it must have an explicit intuitive referent that presentationally displays the metric relations discursively expressed in it causes problems. For the intuitive element is just the one that men as knowers, even by Kant's own lights, cannot self-motivatedly control. If they could, then any possible mathematical proposition could be made true, except of course logically self-contradictory ones. Consequently, Kant's theory that space is a metaphysically necessary condition of man's apprehension of objects as outer, that it is the pure form of outer intuition, is inadequate to secure the property of mathematical truths he was most concerned with, certainty. It remains a theory that leaves man as knower passive in relation to the *subject matter* of mathematics and consequently succumbs to all the pitfalls of that circumstance. The most that Kant can claim is that his metaphysics of space and time can account for the possibility of synthetic a priori propositions in the full sense he sets out in the Introduction, but not that it guarantees that men can be certain that any such proposition is in fact true. I, therefore, feel justified in saying that one part of Kant's Copernican Revolution in philosophy fails: Given this theory of the origin of space, men cannot have the kind of insight into what the mind produces from itself that affords certainty about space's metric.

NOTES

1. All references to the *Kritik der reinen Vernunft* will be to the edition by Raymond Schmidt (Hamburg: Verlag von Felix Meiner, PhB 37 a, 1956). Page numbers will be cited in the usual way, A standing for the edition of 1781 and B for that of 1787, and will be placed in parentheses following the citation. All other references to Kant's work will be to: Immanuel Kant, *Kant's gesammelte Schriften,* hrsg., Preussische Akademie der Wissenschaften (28 vols.; Berlin and Leipzig: G. Reimer and Walter de Gruyter and Co., 1901–). Citations will be placed in parentheses in the text. Translations, except where specifically noted, are my own.

2. The most recent discussions of the second edition Preface from this point of view are: Lewis White Beck, *Early German Philosophy* (Cambridge: Harvard, The Belknap Press, 1969), pp. 473-74; P. F. Strawson, *The Bounds of Sense* (London: Methuen, 1966), pp. 43-44; S. Morris Engel, "Kant's Copernican Analogy: A Re-examination," *Kant-Studien* 53 (1961-62): 243-51; James Willard Oliver, "Kant's Copernican Analogy: An Examination of a Re-examination," *Kant-Studien* 55 (1964): pp. 505-11; Norwood Russell Hanson, "Copernicus' Role in Kant's Revolution," *Journal of the History of Ideas* 20 (1959): 274-81; Carl J. Friedrich, ed., *The Philosophy of Kant* (New York: Modern Library, 1949), pp. xxvii-xxviii. Kant's mentions of Copernicus in the second edition Preface are discussed in all standard English language commentaries: Ewing, Paton, Smith, Weldon, Wolff, etc. Only Caird seems not to have been bothered by the problem, a trait he shares with most nineteenth-century commentators, English, German, and French. Engel's paper provides good bibliographical details of the discussion, although it unfortunately omits mention of Hanson's views, inclusion of which would have strengthened its conclusions. The only analyses of Kant's references to Copernicus that focus on their broader context and therefore their methodological implications are in Friedrich, Hanson, and Beck. But even these fail to pursue the methodological implications of the second edition Preface on which I concentrate; consequently, they do not examine the analogy as a strategy to secure conclusions about the nature of the necessity and certainty of human knowledge.

3. This is not the only instance in which a premise necessary to Kant's argumentation remains implicit, even while he is working on an argument. An even more elegant example occurs in the Transcendental Doctrine of Elements, namely, the doctrine that relations cannot affect sensibility. Kant expresses this view in *Träume eines Geistersehers* (AA 2, 344), but never reiterates or explicitly argues for it in his exposition of the Critical doctrine, even though the premise is necessary to its argument. For further details on this issue see my "The Historical and Conceptual Relations between Kant's Metaphysics of Space and Philosophy of Geometry," *Journal of the History of Philosophy* 11 (1973): 483-512 passim, but esp. 489, n. 13.

4. Just how much thought Kant actually devoted to how he should initially acquaint his reader with his intentions in and the fundamental point of view of the *Kritik* is very difficult to determine. The vast bulk of the evidence is negative: By the time he wrote the *Prolegomena* he had not paid much attention to the issue. Only the very slightest hint, in the opening paragraphs of the *Prolegomena* (AA 4,

255-57), suggests that Kant had in 1783 begun to work out an analogy between the proper methods of mathematics and natural science on the one hand and metaphysics on the other. But all he does there is express the view dominating the first paragraph of the second edition Preface, namely, that metaphysics appears previously not to have entered on the path of a science. In other respects, particularly in its emphasis on pure reason's internal unity and the use of architectural metaphors, as well as the contention that metaphysical concepts require a critique and deduction, not a geneology, the opening comments of the *Prolegomena* more closely resemble the first edition Preface than the second. (Incidentally, David W. Tarbet has done an admirable job of discussing Kant's use of metaphor in the *Kritik;* his paper, "The Fabric of Metaphor in Kant's *Critique of Pure Reason,*" *Journal of the History of Philosophy* 6 (1968): 257-70, was of considerable help to me in coming to understand the Prefaces of the *Kritik.*) The *Nachlass* provides no clues as to when Kant might have developed the strategy of the opening paragraphs of the second edition Preface. Hence, it seems almost as if Kant arose one day and in a fit of inspiration just sat down and wrote it.

5. Two points need to be made here, one systematic, the other historical: (a) Systematically, Kant writes that "systematic unity is what first makes ordinary cognition science, i.e., makes a system of a mere aggregate of cognitions" (A832/B860). In clarification of this comment he writes: "I understand by 'System' the unity of a manifold of cognitions in accordance with an idea. This idea is the rational concept of the form of a whole, so far as by means of it the compass of the manifold as well as the places of the parts relative to one another is determined. The scientific concept of reason contains, therefore, the end and form of the whole that is congruent with this requirement" (A832/B860). (b) Historically, from the time Kant was himself able to see the ramifications of his critical epistemology and metaphysics, the idea of presenting his entire theory as a science concerned him greatly. As the critical corpus began to expand, it became increasingly important to him that he make readers realize that in the *Kritik der reinen Vernunft* and the writings for which it formed the basis they were dealing with a totally integrated, scientific philosophy. One finds a growing tendency on Kant's part to emphasize the scientific character of his thought. This begins in the *Prolegomena,* increases in subsequent works, especially the *Grundlegung* and *Metaphysische Anfangsgründe der Naturwissenschaften,* and culminates, at least during the 1780s, in the second edition Preface to the *Kritik.* However, the extremist emphasis Kant gave this issue was in

the first unpublished Introduction to the *Kritik der Urteilskraft.*

6. In this passage Kant neither mentions nor leaves room for alternative and what may very well have been more generally held views of logic, particularly the Aristotelian view that the categories and logical forms are abstracted from man's encounter with the world. Nor does Kant mention the views of his rationalist and empiricist predecessors. Failure to mention rationalist views may have been compatible with his view. But a more general explanation of this failure might be that Kant was assuming the truth of his analysis in the Transcendental Analytic already set out in 1781, and just passed over alternative views. One must also remember that one is dealing with a Preface, which does place restrictions on what might be said. Although I do not agree with it in some major respects, Felix Grayeff's analysis of Kant's reform of logic is germane to what Kant says in the Preface. See *Kant's Theoretical Philosophy,* David Wallford, trans., (New York: Barnes & Nobel, 1970), pp. 20-22, 90-95.

7. Kant's characterization of logic here best conforms to what he describes as pure general logic at A52/B76—A54/B78. One must remember that on final analysis the content of pure general logic derives from transcendental logic, according to Kant.

8. I use representation *(Vorstellung)* to mean any occurrent object of consciousness, be it pure or empirical, intuitive or conceptual, but never a mental act. This is wholly in keeping with Kant's usage, for in his lexicon, the term is the broadest mental object term. See A320/B376.

9. Discussion of Kant's theory of the sources of a priori knowledge in dispositional terms might lead to some problems, especially when one has in mind the sources of logical and categorical organization; however, I do not think it need lead to anything insidious even there, so long as one is careful. Moreover, Kant does suggest it with his notions of original apperception (B132-34) and understanding (see, e.g., A78/B103, B150-52, A326/B383). One feels a great deal more comfortable describing outer and inner sense in this way, because they organize empirical contents deriving from sensation automatically. Henry Allison gives some independent reasons for considering the pure forms of space and time and, I would assume, outer and inner sense as dispositions. See *The Kant-Eberhardt Controversy* (Baltimore: The Johns Hopkins University Press, 1974), pp. 84-88. The issue about space in particular will be central to the second part of this paper.

10. Passages that justify the ascription of this view to Kant include A346/B404—A347/B405, A76/B102—A79/B105, B129-30, B135,

B137, B151-2, A137/B176–A142/B181, and in general any passage in which Kant says that an occurrent representation is or derives from a subjective condition of awareness. Passages alluding specifically to space and time, inner and outer sense, include A42/B59–A43/B60, A26/B42–A28/B44, A32/B49–A36/B53.

11. I believe this notion of self-motivatedness in the development of mathematical concepts (and, as we shall soon see, scientific hypotheses) is expressed in Kant's *Prize Essay* by the adjective *"willkürliche."* It expresses the idea that, while not necessarily arbitrary, these concepts originate in acts of the thinker. See AA 2, 276; A729/B757; AA 4, 321-22; Lewis White Beck, "Kant's Theory of Definition" in *Studies in the Philosophy of Kant* (Indianapolis: Bobbs-Merrill, 1965), pp. 68-69, and my "Historical and Conceptual Relations . . .," pp. 486-87. I must make another point here: The term "knower" has to serve a kind of strange role in this paper. Kant's whole theory in the first half of the *Kritik* is, of course, about the active role the mind plays in knowing. But one must distinguish among kinds of activity. On the one hand, the dispositions that imbue the matter of sensation with spatio-temporal form are active, but not under the control of the knowing subject. On the other, Kant suggests that original apperception as an act of pure spontaneity may very well be under the control of the knowing subject, but that is at least a debatable issue, and I want to avoid it at present. By "knower" in this and similar contexts I mean the subject who stands in a kind of middle ground, both conscious and yet able to exercise control over the content and occurrence of representations present to it. It exercises will and is not identifiable with dispositions, which, while active, are not under one's control as to when they function or what the actual content of the occurrent representations they produce is.

12. Whether this aspect of mathematical knowledge resembles technically or morally practical knowledge more closely is difficult to determine. It seems to resemble technically practical knowledge more because at least some restrictions relevant to the actual existence of the object are placed on mathematics from a source other than the act of conception, namely, the media in which its objects must be constructed, space and time. Morally practical concepts seem not to have extraconceptual restrictions placed on the existence of their objects.

13. Kant held in the *Prize Essay* of 1764 that construction in accordance with concepts that are the products of self-motivated thinking activity is a sufficient explanation of mathematical certainty. There he did not make the genetic apriority of space and time part of his theory of mathematical certainty, much less a necessary condition for it, and I

believe he was correct in this. For further discussion of this issue and other persons' views on it see my paper, "Historical and Conceptual Relations," passim. Precisely what the latter doctrine adds to his theory of mathematical knowledge will be discussed in the second part of this paper. There I deal specifically with Hintikka's and Beth's views concerning the development and nature of Kant's theory of mathematical method and truth.

14. For further information concerning Kant's theory of the nature of hypotheses and their role in scientific investigation, see Robert E. Butts's articles in *Archiv für Geschichte der Philosophie,* "Hypothesis and Explanation in Kant's Philosophy of Science" 43 (1961): 153-70, and "Kant on Hypotheses in the 'Doctrine of Method' and the Logik," ibid. 44 (1962): 185-204. Neither of these papers has anything to say about hypotheses comprising a distinctively a priori aspect of Kant's theory of empirical science. The paper by Robert S. Hartmann, "Kant's Science of Metaphysics and the Scientific Method," *Kant-Studien* 63 (1972), also makes a contribution to this topic.

15. The issue of the contingency or necessity and the certainty of geometrical propositions will be the focus of the second part of this paper.

16. These comments extend to Kant's theory of aesthetic judgments in the *Kritik der Urteilskraft,* even though I cannot consider this fact here.

17. I have covered in detail the development of Kant's philosophy of mathematical knowledge in "Historical and Conceptual Relations," pp. 483-500.

18. B41. This is also the essence of the doctrine that space is transcendentally ideal, a doctrine Kant had formulated in essence in his *Inaugural Dissertation.* See A26/B42–A28/B44, A34/B53, AA 2, 406, and AA 8, 221–23.

19. This position is very similar to the one Allison takes in the *Kant-Eberhardt Controversy,* pp. 84-88. However, it differs in at least this respect: I believe that Kant holds it possible for space and time to be present to consciousness independently of all conceptualization–see B160-1 n. and AA 4, 321–and that in so appearing they can be regarded as pure forms of intuition. Pure forms of intuition should not be labeled, as Allison does, dispositions. Rather, outer and inner sense, so far as the latter are their sources, should be considered the dispositions.

20. This translation is P. G. Lucas's. The distinction Kant makes here between mere homogeneous space devoid of clues about its metric properties, and space as unified by means of concepts originating in,

but not necessarily pure concepts of, the understanding, is the same distinction he makes between space and time as *pure forms of intuition* and *formal intuition* at B160-1. However, Kant does not seem to use this distinction consistently throughout the *Kritik;* the latter term in particular does not seem to be used in other passages the way it is in the one cited.

21. This kind of criticism was leveled at Kant in other contexts by the Classical German Idealists and also, in a very similar context, by Hans Reichenbach in *The Philosophy of Space and Time,* trans. Maria Reichenbach and John Freund (New York: Dover Publications, 1957), pp. 37-58.

22. It would be unfair not to note one advantage that attends passivity, namely, that those aspects toward which men feel passive tend to be the ones to which they ascribe some sort of independent actuality.

INDEX

Affection, empirical 38; transcendental 38.
Analyticity, criterion of 11.
Anthropology 84, 85, 86; practical 66, 67.
Antinomies of pure reason 116, 117.
Appearances in themselves 32, 33, 34, 35, 36, 37, 39, 40, 47, 48, 49; their distinction from appearances 42.
Apriority, genetic 152, 154; logical 152, 153, 154.

Categorical imperative 73.
Causality, mechanical 136, 137; natural 94; through design 136; through freedom 94, 137, 138.
Causal relation 11.
Cognition, mathematical 164.
Concepts, mathematical 158, 159; constructability of 16; priority of pure 158.
Consent, doctrine of 78.
Copernican revolution 149-75.
Corpuscular philosophy 121.
Culture 98.

Design intrinsic in nature 138.
Desire, faculty of 68, 72, 74.
Dispositions, natural 77.

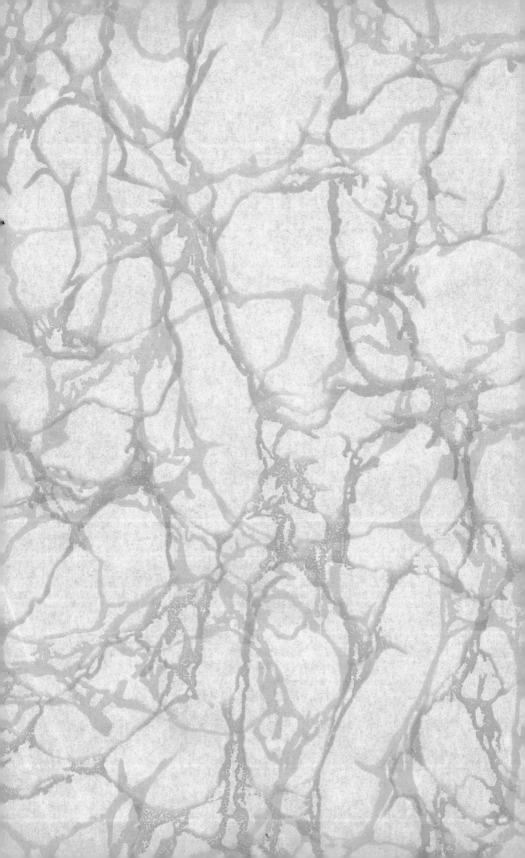